Holiday Entertaining For Dummies®

Cheat Sheet

Tasks You Can Do a Day Ahead

- ✔ Arrange the flowers.
- ✔ Set up the bar.
- ✔ Refrigerate beverages; check your ice supply.
- ✔ Set the table.
- ✔ Make a seating plan and place cards.
- ✔ Set out serving utensils and dishes.
- ✔ Buy perishables.
- ✔ Prepare and refrigerate vegetables and the salad.
- ✔ Set up the coffee machine and cups.
- ✔ Fill the salt and pepper shakers.
- ✔ Cook everything that can possibly be cooked in advance and reheated.

How to Make Your Party Shine

- ✔ Invite a diverse group of guests.
- ✔ Seat dynamic, vivacious, gregarious people at the heads of tables.
- ✔ Greet each guest as though he or she is the one person in the world you most wanted to see.
- ✔ Turn down the lights and burn candles.
- ✔ Decorate with masses of one element (flowers, fruit, candles, cookies, and so on).
- ✔ Play music.
- ✔ Serve exotic cocktails.
- ✔ Serve the very freshest food.
- ✔ Offer more than one dessert.
- ✔ Make or buy something for gue

D1005353

...For Dummies: Bestselling Book Series for Beginners

Holiday Entertaining For Dummies®

Cheat Sheet

Recipe Reading Checklist

- ✔ Read through the recipe at least twice to make sure that you understand the directions.
- ✔ Check that you have all the necessary equipment and ingredients.
- ✔ Make sure that you have enough time to prepare and cook the recipe.
- ✔ Check whether you can (or need to) make any part of the recipe ahead of time.
- ✔ Check whether you need to use an ingredient, such as butter or oil, at different stages in the recipe so that you don't make the mistake of using that ingredient all at once.
- ✔ Check the yield of the recipe and figure out how much you need to make in order to feed your guests.

Common Conversions

Ingredient equivalents

1 cup = 16 tablespoons = 8 ounces

2 cups = 1 pint

2 pints = 1 quart

3 teaspoons = 1 tablespoon

2 tablespoons = 1 ounce

4 tablespoons = ¼ cup

5 tablespoons + 1 teaspoon = ⅓ cup

Temperature conversions

°F	°C
250	120
275	135
300	150
325	160
350	175
375	190
400	205
425	220
450	230

...For Dummies: Bestselling Book Series for Beginners

HOLIDAY ENTERTAINING FOR DUMMIES®

Edited by

Elizabeth Netedu Kuball

IDG Books Worldwide, Inc.
An International Data Group Company

Foster City, CA ✦ Chicago, IL ✦ Indianapolis, IN ✦ New York, NY

Holiday Entertaining For Dummies®

Published by
IDG Books Worldwide, Inc.
An International Data Group Company
919 E. Hillsdale Blvd.
Suite 400
Foster City, CA 94404
http://www.idgbooks.com (IDG Books Worldwide Web Site)
http://www.dummies.com (Dummies Press Web Site)

Library of Congress Catalog Card No.: 99-66377

ISBN: 0-7645-5235-X

Printed in the United States of America

10 9 8 7 6 5 4 3 2

1O/SZ/QT/QQ/IN

Distributed in the United States by IDG Books Worldwide, Inc.

Distributed by CDG Books Canada Inc. for Canada; by Transworld Publishers Limited in the United Kingdom; by IDG Norge Books for Norway; by IDG Sweden Books for Sweden; by IDG Books Australia Publishing Corporation Pty. Ltd. for Australia and New Zealand; by TransQuest Publishers Pte Ltd. for Singapore, Malaysia, Thailand, Indonesia, and Hong Kong; by Gotop Information Inc. for Taiwan; by ICG Muse, Inc. for Japan; by Intersoft for South Africa; by Eyrolles for France; by International Thomson Publishing for Germany, Austria and Switzerland; by Distribuidora Cuspide for Argentina; by LR International for Brazil; by Galileo Libros for Chile; by Ediciones ZETA S.C.R. Ltda. for Peru; by WS Computer Publishing Corporation, Inc., for the Philippines; by Contemporanea de Ediciones for Venezuela; by Express Computer Distributors for the Caribbean and West Indies; by Micronesia Media Distributor, Inc. for Micronesia; by Chips Computadoras S.A. de C.V. for Mexico; by Editorial Norma de Panama S.A. for Panama; by American Bookshops for Finland.

For general information on IDG Books Worldwide's books in the U.S., please call our Consumer Customer Service department at 800-762-2974. For reseller information, including discounts and premium sales, please call our Reseller Customer Service department at 800-434-3422.

For information on where to purchase IDG Books Worldwide's books outside the U.S., please contact our International Sales department at 317-596-5530 or fax 317-572-4002.

For consumer information on foreign language translations, please contact our Customer Service department at 1-800-434-3422, fax 317-572-4002, or e-mail rights@idgbooks.com.

For information on licensing foreign or domestic rights, please phone +1-650-653-7098.

For sales inquiries and special prices for bulk quantities, please contact our Order Services department at 800-434-3422 or write to the address above.

For information on using IDG Books Worldwide's books in the classroom or for ordering examination copies, please contact our Educational Sales department at 800-434-2086 or fax 317-572-4005.

For press review copies, author interviews, or other publicity information, please contact our Public Relations department at 650-653-7000 or fax 650-653-7500.

For authorization to photocopy items for corporate, personal, or educational use, please contact Copyright Clearance Center, 222 Rosewood Drive, Danvers, MA 01923, or fax 978-750-4470.

About the Authors

Ray Foley: A former Marine with over 20 years of bartending and restaurant experience, Ray Foley is the author of *Bartending For Dummies,* published by IDG Books Worldwide, Inc. Foley is also the founder and publisher of *BARTENDER* magazine (www.bartender.com), the only magazine in the world specifically geared toward bartenders and one of the very few primarily designed for servers of alcohol.

Christopher Hobbs, L.Ac.: A fourth-generation herbalist and botanist, Christopher Hobbs is the author of *Herbal Remedies For Dummies,* published by IDG Books Worldwide, Inc., and has over 30 years of experience with herbs. In 1989, he founded the American School of Herbalism in Santa Cruz, California (with Michael Tierra, O.M.D., L.Ac.) to educate professionals and laypersons in the safe use of medicinal plants.

Bryan Miller: Bryan Miller is a former restaurant critic and feature writer for *The New York Times,* who also wrote *Cooking For Dummies* (with Marie Rama) and *Desserts For Dummies* (with Bill Yosses), published by IDG Books Worldwide, Inc. He has also written eight other books on cooking. Miller is the recipient of the James Beard Who's Who Food and Beverage Award, which recognizes outstanding achievement in the field of food and wine.

Marie Rama: An independent food, beverage, and media consultant, Marie Rama wrote *Cooking For Dummies* (with Bryan Miller), published by IDG Books Worldwide, Inc. Rama has worked as a professional pastry chef and recipe developer for several food companies and associations.

Linda Smith: Having dreamed of being a writer since the age of nine when she got her first rejection slip from *Reader's Digest,* Linda Smith is the coauthor of *Entertaining For Dummies* (with Suzanne Williamson), published by IDG Books Worldwide, Inc. Smith, who is a freelance writer, met Suzanne Williamson on the tennis court, where the seeds of a book on entertaining were planted.

Janet Sobesky: The author of *Household Hints For Dummies,* Janet Sobesky is the Home Design and Lifestyle Editor for *Woman's Day* magazine, where she also edits the incredibly popular "Tip Talk" feature. She appears frequently on radio and television shows such as *Good Morning America* and the Discovery Channel's *Home Matters* as an expert on household maintenance, organization, and decorating.

Suzanne Williamson: Having lectured on entertaining to over 10,000 people from all over the world, Suzanne Williamson is the coauthor of *Entertaining For Dummies* (with Linda Smith), published by IDG Books Worldwide, Inc. Some of her clients have included the Food and Wine Institute, Ford Motor Company, General Electric, and Templeton Fund Worldwide.

Bill Yosses: For ten years, Bill Yosses was the pastry chef at the four-star *(The New York Times)* Bouley Restaurant in Manhattan. The coauthor of *Desserts For Dummies* (with Bryan Miller), published by IDG Books Worldwide, Inc., Yosses trained at a number of top bakeries and restaurants in Paris, including Fauchon, La Maison du Chocolat, and Le Notre Pastry School.

Publisher's Acknowledgments

We're proud of this book; please register your comments through our IDG Books Worldwide Online Registration Form located at http://my2cents.dummies.com.

Some of the people who helped bring this book to market include the following:

Acquisitions, Editorial, and Media Development

Editor: Elizabeth Netedu Kuball

Acquisitions Editor: Holly McGuire

Editorial Coordinator: Michelle Vukas

Editorial Director: Kristin A. Cocks

Editorial Assistant: Anita C. Snyder

Production

Project Coordinator: Melissa Stauffer

Layout and Graphics: Angela F. Hunckler, Brent Savage, Kathie Schutte

Proofreader: Brian Massey

Indexer: Sharon Hilgenberg

Special Help: Beth Parlon

General and Administrative

IDG Books Worldwide, Inc.: John Kilcullen

IDG Books Technology Publishing Group: Richard Swadley, Senior Vice President and Publisher; Walter Bruce III, Vice President and Associate Publisher; Steven Sayre, Associate Publisher; Joseph Wikert, Associate Publisher; Mary Bednarek, Branded Product Development Director; Mary Corder, Editorial Director

IDG Books Consumer Publishing Group: Roland Elgey, Senior Vice President and Publisher; Kathleen A. Welton, Vice President and Publisher; Kevin Thornton, Acquisitions Manager; Kristin A. Cocks, Editorial Director

IDG Books Internet Publishing Group: Brenda McLaughlin, Senior Vice President and Publisher; Diane Graves Steele, Vice President and Associate Publisher; Sofia Marchant, Online Marketing Manager

IDG Books Production for Dummies Press: Debbie Stailey, Associate Director of Production; Cindy L. Phipps, Manager of Project Coordination, Production Proofreading, and Indexing; Tony Augsburger, Manager of Prepress, Reprints, and Systems; Laura Carpenter, Production Control Manager; Shelley Lea, Supervisor of Graphics and Design; Debbie J. Gates, Production Systems Specialist; Robert Springer, Supervisor of Proofreading; Kathie Schutte, Production Supervisor

Dummies Packaging and Book Design: Patty Page, Manager, Promotions Marketing

♦

The publisher would like to give special thanks to Patrick J. McGovern, without whom this book would not have been possible.

♦

Table of Contents

Introduction

• •

*S*omehow, what with all the jam-packed shopping malls, ungodly credit card bills, and sleep deprivation, most of us have forgotten that the holidays are supposed to be a time of great fun. "Yeah, yeah, yeah," you say, "I've heard it all before. Peace on earth, good will to men."

Before you turn into a scrooge, check out this book. Here you'll find suggestions for getting organized for your holiday party, cooking the perfect meal no matter who your guests may be, and a multitude of other common holiday problems. With this book at your fingertips, you can focus your attention on the good stuff, instead of dwelling on the stress.

Why You Need This Book

You need this book because your life is so full of friends, family, and commitments that you don't have much time to entertain throughout the year. But when the holidays arrive, even if you're not gung ho on the thought of throwing a party, you may be expected to. This book helps you get through it with grace, and it reminds you that the holidays should be, above all, fun.

How to Use This Book

If you're sitting down with a cup of coffee while visions of sugarplums are dancing in your kids' heads, feel free to read from start to finish. But if you're pressed for time (and who isn't during the holidays?), skip to the part that you need most. Write in the book, highlight it, or give it to your sister with a note attached saying, "Christmas at *your* house this year."

How This Book Is Organized

This book is divided into three parts. The first two cover entertaining and cooking, in that order. And if you don't know the meaning of the word *time,* check out Part III for some quick and easy suggestions for surviving it all.

Part I: Entertaining like You Do It All the Time

During the holiday season, most of us are faced with entertaining at least once. And if your idea of entertaining is ordering a pizza and sitting the kids in front of the TV with a movie, then you've come to the right place. Chapter 1 guides you through the process of figuring out what kind of party you want to have, deciding whom you want to invite, making your guest list, and inviting the people lucky enough to be on it. In Chapter 2, you get organized for the big day. We fill you in on making the right lists to be sure you're prepared, planning the timing from beginning to end, creating the right atmosphere, and setting up your bar. We even help you get ready for a spur-of-the-moment party — the most stressful of them all! Chapter 3 focuses on the day of your holiday shindig — everything from setting the table to being a good host. Whatever your entertaining questions may be, we have the quick and easy answers here.

Part II: Cooking Up a Storm

The chapters in this part guide you through the preparation of the food for your party. Whether you're making a traditional Thanksgiving dinner for the first time or you're looking for a special recipe for your vegetarian niece who's visiting for the holidays, we have just the recipes for you. In this part, you discover tried-and-true recipes, as well as some new and exciting ones to add to your menu. We even give you some great suggestions for popular drinks. This part gives you guidance in the kitchen and beyond — everything from appetizers to salads, dinners to desserts — so you can *enjoy* your holiday party rather than being relegated to the kitchen and worrying about what to make.

Part III: The Part of Tens

If you have only five minutes to spare, check out one of the chapters in this part. We give you suggestions for ten quick things you can do to clean up your house for surprise guests and ten herbal remedies for common holiday ailments. You want survival strategies? We've got 'em here.

Icons Used in This Book

Throughout this book are little pictures called *icons,* which highlight important information. Here's the decoder key:

This icon points out suggestions for ways to do things better or faster. If you're looking for some quick and easy pointers on ways to improve your holidays, check out the paragraphs with this icon by their side.

 This icon is a friendly reminder of information you may already know or ideas you may want to keep in mind as you make your way from Thanksgiving to the New Year.

 Don't be scared by this icon — but do pay attention to it. In these paragraphs, you'll discover information on ways to avoid mishaps and minor catastrophes.

 If you're in a hurry to gather the basics, skip paragraphs adorned by this icon. Don't get us wrong . . . the information in these paragraphs is great to know. In fact, it may even serve as great conversation for the next holiday cocktail party and help you impress your family and friends. But it isn't crucial, so if you have to skip anything, skip these paragraphs.

Where to Go from Here

Decide what matters most to you, and flip to that part of the book. Or start right in with Chapter 1. Focus on one task at a time, instead of getting overwhelmed by all the things you have to do. By following a few of the easy suggestions in the pages ahead, you can make this year's holiday season one filled with joy — or at least free of stress!

Part I

Entertaining like You Do It All the Time

The 5th Wave   By Rich Tennant

OVER PLANNING A PARTY

"At 1700 hours position yourselves along the perimeter of the living room. As they enter we'll hit them with the nuts and bread sticks. At 1750 hours Dolores will move to their right flank and advance with the drinks, driving them from the kitchen. As they weaken from dancing we'll cut off their supplies and force them into the driveway."

In this part...

*I*n this part, we we break down your party into simple, manageable parts. You figure out how to get organized, put together a winning guest list, and make an offer your family and friends can't refuse.

We help you figure out how to plan in advance by setting the table, creating the right atmosphere, and knowing how to be a good host. But we also give you tips for planning for a spur-of-the-moment party with grace and style.

If you're having a party and you're not sure where to start, look no further.

Chapter 1

So You Want to Entertain

In This Chapter

▶ Figuring out what kind of party to have

▶ Choosing your guests

▶ Determining how much space you have to work with

▶ Setting a date

▶ Inviting your guests

*I*f you've decided to have a party, but your mind hasn't made it past that point, you've come to the right place. This chapter gets you started thinking about the who, what, where, when, why, and how of entertaining. You'll determine the kind of party you want, select the guests, figure out where you'll have it, set a date, and start the invitation process — all in this one little chapter! So what are you waiting for?

Deciding What Kind of Party to Have

At most parties, all anyone really expects is a few hours of fun. But when the holidays roll around, expectations fill the air about food, drink, dress, decorations, behavior, and more. For this reason, holidays can be a considerable source of anguish.

The difference in what works and what doesn't, what comforts and what causes exhaustion, what astonishes and what disappoints is all in the expectations. Start with your own. Do you expect to prepare holiday dinners for your family plus have a holiday party for your friends? Do you really expect to grow your own pumpkins, bake from scratch, chop down the Christmas tree, make the decorations, and shop for the gifts, all while looking glamorous and being pleasant? Pleeeeze! Give yourself a break. Most people feel highly accomplished if they just get the presents wrapped, much less prepare meals for their families and entertain everyone else, too.

Take a look at the following sections to narrow and define your goals a bit.

Figuring out and focusing on the real reason you're throwing a party

The first step toward an enjoyable holiday season is taking a look at why you're throwing a party in the first place. And you do that by figuring out what's most important to you. Do you have the time and energy for a special family gathering, a big lavish party, *and* a private celebration with a friend? Can you handle it all, or do you need to make choices? Is it more important to make the pumpkin pie from scratch, or would one from the bakery give you more time to spend with your family? Is it more important for your tree to be perfect or for your children to have fun decorating it?

Many things are beyond our control during the holidays. The one thing you *can* control, however, is yourself — your attitude, how you spend your time, and with whom you spend it. Once a year, we have this marvelous chance to take a trip back in time, to revisit people and places of the past. We also have the opportunity to create new memories for ourselves, our families, and our friends.

 Instead of being bound by expectations (yours and everyone else's), turn your holiday entertaining into one great big opportunity. Use it to

> ✔ Discover your family history.

> ✔ Explore old traditions and create new ones.

> ✔ Spend time with the people who matter to you the most.

Remembering tradition as you plan your holiday shindig

A big part of the holiday madness revolves around the expectations of different generations. Every family has its own set of annual rituals or traditions. You can either kill yourself trying to do it the way it's always been done, revolt and go on a major guilt trip, or find a way to compromise so that everyone gets what he or she wants and needs. The trick is to figure out exactly which traditions are worth the trouble to preserve and which ones you can alter or eliminate.

Sometimes a problem begins when you need to blend different sets of traditions. Today's expanded families often combine different cultures, religions, and ethnic backgrounds. Find out which traditions mean the most to your loved ones, and try to include some of everyone's favorites.

While you are busy blending, banishing, and/or preserving the old, you may want to create a few traditions of your own. Incorporate a family activity or a favorite food — something to make your celebration unique and to pass on to the next generation.

Duck, Duck, Goose: Figuring Out Whom to Invite

Most people invite particular guests for one of the following reasons:

- ✓ They always invite the same people.
- ✓ They need to pay back invitations.
- ✓ They want something from one of the guests.

Although there is nothing wrong with using entertaining to pay back invitations or get on the good side of someone, making a guest list can encompass so much more.

Setting your priorities

If you normally use the methods listed earlier in this section to determine your guest list, try a new approach. Instead of going outside and inviting people for an ulterior motive, turn inward. Ask yourself these questions:

- ✔ Who matters to me?
- ✔ Who makes me happy?
- ✔ Who is supportive of me?
- ✔ Who is fun to be around?
- ✔ Who intrigues me?
- ✔ Who do I want to know better?

Gather these people around you, and your party is refreshing and exciting. People are not just feeding on your food, but feasting on each other's personalities, charm, and energy.

Looking at how many people you can invite

Many factors affect the number of guests you can accommodate. First consider what kind of party you are giving and how much space you have. Be realistic about your energy level, too. Inviting many guests is much more draining than inviting only a few.

No exact formula exists for inviting the right or wrong number of guests to any party. However, some numbers just seem to work better than others. Take a look at the following suggestions, but keep in mind that the numbers we suggest here are general guidelines. Use them to help you figure out what you can handle and what works best for you.

- ✔ **Dinner parties:** For a sit-down dinner party, seven is an ideal number. (That's six guests plus you, or five plus you and your spouse or date.) This doesn't mean that you need to cancel your plans if you have only six or panic if the total is eight. You can have a wonderful dinner party with five, six, eight, or more people around a table.

Seven people around one table can have one conversation. With eight or more, guests tend to talk only to the people directly to their left and right.

✔ **Large parties:** A large party can be defined as too many people to fit around your dining room table or too many people to fit in your house. To determine how many guests to invite to a large party, ask yourself:

- Will the guests be sitting, standing, or both? If you are not serving a sit-down meal, you probably have space for more guests.

- What ages are the guests? Younger guests won't mind as much if they are crowded together or have to stand. If your guests are older, be sure that you have enough places for them to sit and space to move around without being bumped from every direction.

- Do the guests all know each other? If so, make it a crowd. If not, allow for a little more personal space.

For large parties, the usual turnout is 80 percent. If you want to have 50 guests attending your party, invite 60 to allow for the 20 percent who won't come.

✔ **Cocktail parties:** There is no ideal number of guests to invite to a cocktail party. A small cocktail party can be charming with as few as eight guests. A large cocktail party can be exhilarating with as many as 25, 50, or 75 guests. You can have a cocktail party to suit any size crowd.

The average length of a cocktail party is between 2 and 2½ hours. Don't invite more guests than you can talk to during the course of the evening; 50 to 75 guests is a good limit. Unless you are an experienced politician, don't expect to get around to talking to 100 guests.

✔ **Buffets:** For a buffet, be sure that you provide enough space for guests to sit comfortably. This does not necessarily mean that they all have to sit at a table or in a plush chair with arms. Guests can be comfortable sitting on pillows on the floor or perched on foot stools, banisters, or stairs. If the affair is casual, people can put their plates on their laps, but they should not have to stand and juggle their plates in their hands.

If entertaining is a new venture for you, start small. Two or three guests can make a perfect party. When you become comfortable with a few guests, you can begin giving larger parties.

No matter what kind or size of party you give, never invite an extra person purely for the sake of creating an even number. Odd numbers of people often generate more intriguing conversations than a group of pairs. Unless the extra person has a dynamite personality, a special charm, or something to add to your party, you're better off without him.

Sizing Up Your House: How Much Space You Have to Work With

The key to finding the right space for your party is to match the size of the room (or rooms) with the size of your guest list. Inviting a realistic number of people is the first step to solving all your space problems.

The setting you choose for the number of guests you invite may also depend on the kind of party you decide to give. Different types of parties require different amounts of space. For example, if you are giving a large cocktail party for 25 guests (mostly standing), you need less space than you do for a casual buffet for the same number of guests (seating themselves randomly). You need even more space for a formal buffet or a sit-down dinner.

A 400-square-foot space with furniture can comfortably hold about 30 people standing. You don't need to waste time measuring to the inch, but estimate your space so that you don't end up having to build an addition to the house to handle your party. Set up tables and chairs in advance, if possible.

Using your resources wisely

If you live in a two-room apartment, you may not think that you have space for entertaining, but you do. Even if you eat your meals off the kitchen counter and the sofa doubles as your bed, you can still entertain in your home. The challenge is to make the most of the space you have.

Think of any obscure places that can be converted to party space with a little creative rearranging. For example, make the closet into a bar by stashing its usual contents under the bed, behind the shower curtain, or in the trunk of your car. Or clear out the center of the closet and drape beautiful sheets over the coats and brooms to turn the closet into a cocoon. Use a colored light bulb to make the space look more like a bar and less like a closet. Set up a small mirrored table on which to display the bottles and glasses. The mirror makes the space look larger and adds sparkle.

No dining table? No problem.

✔ Serve all finger food from your countertop.

✔ Set up folding trays for guests to use as mini-tables.

✔ Have guests use their laps to hold plates.

✔ Turn a side table into a dining table by putting a sheet of plywood and a tablecloth on top.

✔ Seat guests on pillows on the floor around your coffee table and dine Asian style.

✔ Purchase a card table that you can stash away when you are not entertaining.

✔ Rent or borrow a table.

If your problem is not the lack of a dining table, but rather the lack of a sideboard or other place to set up the food, serve from the kitchen countertop and/or stovetop. To create more work space, lay a cutting board across your sink or across two open drawers.

Evaluating the seating capacity of your table

If you decide to rent a table, do some advance figuring. Rearrange the furniture if you must. Then measure your clear space and think round, not square. In most cases, round tables are not only more space-efficient but are also more conducive to conversation.

If your space is long and narrow, consider renting a long, skinny table, sometimes referred to as a conference table. To facilitate talking across the table, the ideal width is 18 inches. If an 18-inch table isn't available, use a standard 30-inch wide banquet table. Fill the gap with wide, low centerpieces.

A long narrow table is most effective if you have enough guests to crowd around it, almost elbow to elbow — especially fun for large family feasts and holiday dinners.

If you're a mathematician, you may be able to figure out how many tables you need and how many of what size can fit in your space. But if numbers aren't your strong suit, do some prearranging to make sure that everything fits. Table 1-1 lists standard table shapes and sizes and the number of people you can actually plan to seat at those tables. (Rental companies may not agree with these numbers.)

Table 1-1	Standard Table Sizes
Round tables	*Seating capacity*
36-inch	Seats 4–5
42-inch	Seats 6–7
48-inch	Seats 7–8
60-inch	Seats 8–9
72-inch	Don't use this size. Because of the distance across the table, conversations are limited to the people directly to your right and left.

Rectangle tables	Seating capacity
6-foot	Seats 8–10
8-foot	Seats 10–12

Pay attention to the table legs and the size of the chairs, as well. A pedestal table seats more people than a table with legs. Armchairs obviously take more space than bistro chairs.

Setting a Date

The best day and time for your party depends largely upon your lifestyle and other obligations:

- ✔ **Saturday may be your best bet if you work long hours during the week.** You can spend Friday evening doing preliminary chores and taking some time to unwind from your work week. You have at least part of the day on Saturday to make the final preparations and Sunday to recover. To prepare for a large party without taking a day off from work, keep your plan simple and start far enough ahead so that you can make a few preparations each night.

- ✔ **Friday night may be more convenient if you don't work outside your home and if you have school-age children.** You can get things done while the kids are at school, and they won't have time to wreck the house before your party.

- ✔ **Three-day weekends are a good opportunity for a Sunday afternoon picnic or a Sunday evening dinner, with a cushion of time on both sides for preparation and recovery.**

If your obligations dictate a less-than-convenient day and time, take that fact into account when scheduling your preparations. Adjust the big picture to meet what is a realistic schedule for you or plan far enough in advance to get a head start. For example, if you want to have friends over for dinner on Thursday night, plan a menu you can make ahead. Don't wait until Thursday when you get home from work to start cooking.

Inviting Your Guests

The most appropriate tactic for inviting your guests, whether writing or calling, depends largely on your personality and the type of party you are planning. If the party is formal or very large, send written invitations. Otherwise, the method you choose is entirely up to you.

Verbal invitations are great

- ✔ For spur-of-the-moment gatherings
- ✔ For casual parties or semiformal events
- ✔ When the guest list is subject to change
- ✔ When you want to create immediate excitement

If a verbal invitation is the method you choose, take a look at the following suggestions for when to call based on what kind of party you're having.

Type of party	When to call
Well-planned large party	2–3 weeks in advance
Luncheon or small dinner	7–14 days ahead
Last-minute get-together	The afternoon of the party

Written invitations are preferable

- ✔ For parties planned far in advance
- ✔ For formal affairs
- ✔ When you have a definite guest list
- ✔ When you want to establish a tone or theme

If your party calls for written invitations, take a look at the following guidelines for when to send them.

Type of party	When to mail
Formal dinner	4 weeks ahead
Informal dinner	2–3 weeks ahead
Luncheon or tea	2–3 weeks ahead
Cocktail party	3 weeks ahead
Big bash	4 weeks ahead

Regardless of whether you write or call, be sure to include all the pertinent information in your invitation. Guests need to know who is inviting them to what sort of event, the date, the time, and the place.

Guests also need to know exactly for whom the invitation is intended. This may seem obvious, but it can create confusion. To prevent misunderstandings, address the invitation to the party whom you are inviting. If you are inviting a husband and wife, address it to "Mr. and Mrs." If the children are invited, too, add "and family." If you're having a ladies-only luncheon, then say so in the invitation so that someone doesn't show up with her spouse in tow. In other words, do everything you can to make it crystal clear whose presence is requested.

Give an unmarried person the option of bringing a guest, unless you are inviting him to fill a specific place in your guest list. Otherwise, he may assume that it's okay and bring a date anyway. Or he may wonder if it's okay and hesitate to ask. Extending the courtesy to bring a guest is especially important if you know that he is seeing someone regularly.

Chapter 2

Preparing for the Big Event

Sometimes the greatest stress in throwing a party is opening your home up to guests. You want the house to be neat, clean, and organized — in other words, you want it to look like no one lives there! As hard as it may be, start your holiday season by focusing on the important part: spending time with family and friends. And give your inner perfectionist a break. Then take a deep breath and read this chapter to get organized.

In this chapter, you find everything you need to know on planning ahead. We tell you about three lists that can make your party-planning life much easier. We also show you how to make a timetable of what you'll do and when you'll do it. And we cover things like creating the right atmosphere, getting your bar set up, and handling a spur-of-the-moment party. Use the suggestions in this chapter, and your party will go off without a hitch!

Making a List, Checking It Twice

Making lists is one of the best ways to get and stay organized. The three lists that follow come in handy for any and every kind of party. The items on each list will vary according to the type and the size of the party.

If you're an accomplished host or if your party is small, you may not need to make any lists. As you become more experienced, many of these steps will come naturally. But for large parties or complicated menus, even party professionals rely on detailed lists.

Following are a few reasons why making lists is a good idea:

- ✔ Nothing is left to chance.
- ✔ You can mentally assess everything you're going to be doing.
- ✔ Committing chores to paper is the first step toward getting them done.
- ✔ A written list can be passed to someone else — a child, spouse, roommate, or friend — who offers to help.

The shopping list: Everything you need to buy

Write down your menu and all the ingredients you need to buy. Check your pantry for items you may already have. Also, check your drinks. You may want to separate this list into columns. One side can be your grocery list, and the other side can be miscellaneous items that you must purchase elsewhere. In addition to the ingredients for your menu and bar, your list may include such items as candles, napkins, a mop, and so on.

When you make your final stop for fresh food items on your grocery list, allow some flexibility in your menu. For example, if the asparagus you had planned to serve looks like dead tree branches, buy the gorgeous green broccoli instead.

The task list: Everything you need to do before the day of the party

The task list helps you keep track of what you need to do before the day of the party. For a dinner party or buffet, the list may include some or all of the following: shopping, food preparation, house cleaning, polishing silverware, ordering flowers, decorating, setting the table, and so on.

If you invite friends at the spur of the moment, you can keep your task list in your head. For example, if you ask a few neighbors over to watch a ball game, your task list could be as simple as calling your favorite take-out restaurant, clearing off the sofa, and turning on the TV. For a more formal party or a large crowd, spread your task list out over a longer period of time. Break down each task into segments that can be done quickly or even while you're doing something else. For example, buy the food for your party while you do your regular grocery shopping. Stop by the wine store while you're out running everyday errands. Mix a cake to freeze for the party, and while it bakes, prepare dinner for yourself or your family.

The last-minute to-do list: Everything you have to do the day of the party

Much of your preparation can be done before the day of the party, but some tasks cannot be completed in advance. Divide the day of the party into time segments and make a list including things you need to do in the morning, things to be done later in the day, and only one or two last-minute things to do just before the guests arrive.

No matter what kind of party you are having, this list includes all final preparations. For a dinner or buffet, you can include defrosting food, chopping vegetables, setting up the coffee machine, frosting a cake, setting the table, arranging flowers, and so on. For a big party in a space other than your home, the day-of-the-party list may even include travel, decorating, adjusting lights, and a final meeting with caterers, servers, or entertainers.

Don't forget to include some time to shower, dress, and relax. A few years ago, a friend of ours was giving her first seated dinner party. She loved cooking, so she had planned to serve a complicated menu with many courses. She was so engrossed in preparing the food, she forgot to get ready. When the first guest rang the doorbell, she was wearing a bathrobe with her hair wrapped in a towel.

Timing Is Everything: Creating a Timetable for Your Big Day

To avoid timing problems, expand your day-of-the-party list to include a timetable. A timetable includes all the cooking and serving tasks to be done after the guests arrive.

Creating and referring to a timetable will help you keep everything running smoothly and on time. It can also help ensure that you won't have to serve food incredibly late, which can ruin any party. (Guests get tired as they wonder when they will eat, sometimes drink too much alcohol, and run out of conversations in the interim.)

Making a timetable also helps you have time to spend with your guests. The whole point of inviting guests is to enjoy their company. You defeat the purpose of the party if you are so preoccupied with serving the food that you never get out of the kitchen.

For any type of party, the best way to make your timetable is to work backward. Figure out what time you want people to eat. For example, if you've asked two friends over for drinks and you plan to serve hors d'oeuvres that take 15 minutes to heat, allow enough time to preheat the oven, take the hors d'oeuvres out of the refrigerator or package, heat them, and put them on a serving platter.

By putting everything in writing, you know what to do and when to do it, even if you get distracted or confused. For example, if the ice cream is supposed to be churning while guests are eating, your list may save you the embarrassment of forgetting to start the churn. (By the time you discover your mistake, guests may not want to wait another hour for dessert.)

Keep your timetable in the kitchen and use it like a cheat sheet. Think of it as a tool that allows you to relax and enjoy your guests. By relying on your written time schedule to keep you on task, you can concentrate on conversations and having fun. If you have planned your time well, things will seem to "just happen." Nobody needs to know what went on backstage.

Setting the Mood with Music

Music can be a wonderful addition to a party. You can use it as entertainment or as a simple background effect.

When using music as a background for smaller parties, be careful that it doesn't become overwhelming. It should never be so loud that it interferes with conversation.

Choose music carefully. Consider your guests and the atmosphere you intend to create. Rock 'n' roll may be all right for your New Year's Eve bash, but not necessarily appropriate for a holiday dinner with your in-laws. Use your own taste in music combined with what you know about your guests to create the desired atmosphere.

Classical music is lovely for a special dinner party. In fact, Georg Philipp Telemann wrote music especially for banquets in the first half of the eighteenth century.

For a cocktail party, you can't go wrong with jazz. Actually, jazz is appropriate for almost any party, especially when guests are arriving and during the cocktail hour. Jazz can create a lively atmosphere.

The most spirited and fascinating parties require no music at all. If guests are intrigued by the company, they won't notice the lack of music. A lively party makes its own music, with the harmony of many voices and the steady rhythm of laughter.

Take a moment to listen to your party. Your ears can tell if guests are enjoying themselves and if the party is a raging success.

Don't panic if you hear a lull. Parties generally have a sound pause about a half hour after starting, almost as if the guests are taking a collective deep breath. Although the sound of silence can seem to last forever to the host, it's really only a moment before guests get right back into it. Expect the volume to fluctuate — it's part of the natural noise rhythm of the party.

Setting Up Your Bar

A popular part of many holiday parties are drinks from the bar. And if you're throwing a party, you've probably spent at least a little time worrying that you'll have the drinks your guests will want. If so, you've come to the right place. This section is devoted not only to stocking your bar with alcohol and supplies but also to providing tips on where to set up your bar and how to serve the drinks.

Steering the traffic flow

Keep the bar as far as possible from your food and snacks. This strategy prevents large groups of people from staying in one area. If possible, base a wine and beer bar in one area and a cocktail bar in another.

Keeping your bar in or near the kitchen

Cleaning up spills is a lot easier in your kitchen. What's more, you'll do a lot less running around if you are close to the sink and refrigerator. If you have to set up your bar in another location, put a small rug or cloth under and behind the bar to protect the floor or carpet. And no matter where your bar is, use a strong, steady table to avoid tipping or collapsing.

Serving smartly

Your party will run smoothly and your guests will be happy if you take the following suggestions to heart:

- ✔ Use nothing larger than a shot glass for shots, and do not serve doubles to your guests. You aren't doing anyone any favors by over-serving. If a recipe calls for 1½ ounces of vodka, use just that amount. All mixed drinks should not exceed 2 ounces of liquor.

- ✔ Use lower proof products if they're available.

- ✔ Have alcohol-free drinks available in addition to coffee, tea, and sodas.

- ✔ Use only clean, fresh ice and fruit.

- ✔ If possible, chill glasses and do not put them out until five minutes before the party begins.

- ✔ When serving hot drinks, make sure that the cups or glasses have handles.

- ✔ Use a scoop, tongs, or a large spoon to serve ice. Never use your hands.

- ✔ If you do not have bottle pourers, rub wax paper over the tip of liquor bottles to prevent dripping.

- ✔ Close the bar 1 to 1½ hours before the end of the party.

- ✔ If possible, hire a professional bartender.

Knowing how much liquor to buy

Table 2-1 shows the amount of liquor you should buy for the number of guests at your party. The left column lists the products, and the remaining columns list the number of bottles of that product you should purchase. The last row of the table lists the estimated total costs.

Table 2-1	How Much Liquor to Purchase for a Party			
Product (750-mL bottles)	**10–30 Guests**	**30–40 Guests**	**40–60 Guests**	**60–100 Guests**
White wine, domestic	4	4	6	8
White wine, imported	2	2	2	3
Red wine, domestic	1	2	3	3
Red wine, imported	1	1	2	2
Blush wine	1	2	2	2
Champagne, domestic	2	3	4	4
Champagne, imported	2	2	2	2
Vermouth, extra dry	1	1	2	2
Vermouth, red	1	1	1	1
Vodka	2	3	3	4
Rum	1	2	2	2
Gin	1	2	2	3
Scotch	1	2	2	3
Whiskey, American or Canadian	1	1	2	2
Bourbon	1	1	1	1
Irish whiskey	1	1	1	2
Tequila	2	2	2	3
Brandy/cognac	1	2	2	3

Product (750-mL bottles)	10–30 Guests	30–40 Guests	40–60 Guests	60–100 Guests
Apéritifs (your choice)	1	1	2	2
Cordials (your choice)	3	3	3	3
Beer (12-ounce bottles)	48	72	72	96
Total cost	**$300– $400**	**$400– $550**	**$550– $700**	**$550– $700**

With the exception of beer, the preceding table is based on 1¾ ounces of liquor per drink. Cost totals are in U.S. dollars.

The number of products you purchase will vary depending on the age of the crowd. If a crowd is dominated by people aged 21 to 35, increase by one-half the amount of vodka, rum, tequila, and beer you purchase.

Knowing how many supplies to buy

Your bar needs more than just liquor. Table 2-2 lists the other supplies that you'll have to purchase. Again, the total costs (in U.S. dollars) are listed in the last row.

Table 2-2	Other Bar Supplies			
Product	10–30 Guests	30–40 Guests	40–60 Guests	60–100 Guests
Soda (2-liter bottles)				
Club soda/seltzer water	3	3	4	5
Ginger ale	2	2	2	3
Cola	3	3	3	4
Diet cola	3	3	3	4
Lemon-lime soda	2	3	3	4
Tonic water	2	2	3	3

Product	10–30 Guests	30–40 Guests	40–60 Guests	60–100 Guests
Juices (quarts)				
Tomato	2	2	3	3
Grapefruit	2	2	3	3
Orange	2	2	3	3
Cranberry	2	2	3	3
Miscellaneous items				
Ice (trays)	10	15	20	30
Napkins (dozens)	4	4	6	8
Stirrers (1,000/box)	1	1	1	1
Angostura bitters (bottles)	1	1	1	2
Cream of coconut (cans)	1	2	2	2
Grenadine (bottles)	1	1	1	2
Horseradish (small jars)	1	1	1	2
Lime juice (bottles)	1	1	1	2
Lemons	3	4	5	6
Limes	2	3	3	4
Maraschino cherries (jars)	1	1	1	1
Olives (jars)	1	1	1	1
Oranges	1	2	2	3
Milk (quarts)	1	1	1	2
Mineral water (1-liter) bottles	2	3	4	5
Superfine sugar (boxes)	1	1	1	1
Tabasco Sauce	1	1	1	1
Worcestershire sauce (bottles)	1	1	1	1
Total cost	$30–$40	$40–$45	$45–$50	$50–$55

Organizing a Spur-of-the-Moment Party

Don't let any of these well-laid plans and organizational tips intimidate you or keep you from throwing last-minute parties. Spur-of-the-moment get-togethers are often the most fun. Ninety-nine out of one hundred of these parties are successful. Because expectations are not high (neither yours nor your guests'), great enjoyment comes as a pleasant surprise.

Keep your pantry, freezer, and bar stocked with a few items for drop-in company and last-minute entertaining. Some items you can keep on hand include candles, tablecloths, napkins, champagne, wine, chocolates, nuts, and so on. Use your imagination to make the most of what you have for spur-of-the-moment gatherings:

✔ Throw together some pasta and a simple sauce. Serve it with fruit or whatever you have on hand.

✔ Check your refrigerator for leftovers. Chopped-up meat and vegetables make terrific fillings for crepes, frittatas, omelets, or even bases for soufflés.

✔ If your cupboards are bare, use the telephone. Order takeout and just figure out a place to put it all.

The trick to last-minute entertaining is to organize the time you have and the space around you. Organizing in a short amount of time means you may have to do two or three things at once — hide the clutter under the furniture, dash through the middle of the floor with the vacuum, and unload the dishwasher. You can order take-out food or raid your own pantry or freezer. (Even if you invite people for drinks, they will expect a peanut, an olive, or some morsel of food.)

For instant atmosphere, turn off the telephone ringer, dim the overhead lights, and light a few candles.

When faced with drop-in company or a need to throw together an instant party, take a few minutes to catch your breath. Make up your mind that this last-minute endeavor is fun. Even the best-laid plans are useless if you're so stressed out that you make your guests nervous wrecks.

Chapter 3

The Big Day

So you've made it to the day of the party. This chapter gives you everything you need to know to ensure that your party is fantastic. We take you through the process of setting the table, seating your guests in specific places, being a good host, and keeping your guests busy. Just read this short chapter the morning of your big day, and you'll be able to focus on having a good time instead of worrying about whether your party will be a success.

Setting the Table

One of the more daunting tasks involved in throwing a party may be something as simple as setting the table. You may have a full set of silverware but have no clue where all the forks and spoons go. Or you may be worried that you don't have the silverware you need. Read on! We help you set aside your worries right here.

Figuring out which pieces of silverware you need

Have you ever sat down in a fancy restaurant only to face six forks, four spoons, an entire set of knives, and goblets galore? Each item has its intended function, but all that glass and silver can be a little confusing.

If your dinner requires more than one fork per person and you don't have enough to go around, aim for one apiece and wash them between courses. (Most people don't know what to do with all those extras anyway.)

According to Ed Munves of James Robinson, Inc., in New York (one of the world's most elegant silver stores), "Nothing is wrong as long as it's done neatly, cleanly, and politely. Too much emphasis is put on rituals that had to start with someone making up rules. People should do what is comfortable for them and their guests."

When it comes to utensils, how many you put on the table is insignificant. What counts is that each guest has just what is needed to eat and enjoy the food. The following table shows uses for each utensil.

Utensil	Use
Small fork	First course, salad, breakfast, lunch
Large fork	Lunch, dinner
Large spoon	Soup, dessert
Small spoon	Dessert, fruit, stirring
Knife	Cutting, spreading

For buffets, you can either set the dining table with silverware at each place or set up the utensils on the end of the buffet table. If guests are sitting randomly (or in places other than tables), you can roll up a set of utensils (fork, knife, spoon) inside each napkin. Stand the rolls up in a basket or bowl for a presentation that looks like sculpture.

Knowing where to put the forks, knives, and spoons

After you round up all the plates, silverware, and glasses you need to set your table or tables, your next step is figuring out where it all goes. Know a few basic rules about proper place settings, such as where to put the water glass and the salad fork. Place settings are standardized not just for the sake of having a set of rules, but for everyone's comfort. For example, whether you eat in a five-star restaurant or in someone's home at a sit-down dinner or a buffet, table settings are the same. Any plates in front of you or to your left are yours, and any glasses to your right are yours as well. Set your table in a logical order so that guests are not confused.

All you really need to serve a great sit-down meal is one plate per person; one fork, knife, and spoon per plate; and one all-purpose glass per person.

If your table is crowded, conserve space by using only two utensils: a fork and a knife. You can save more room by putting the napkins under or on top of each person's plate or by draping them over the backs of the chairs. Take out dessert utensils when it's time for dessert.

If you are serving an elaborate meal and have the space and enough silverware, go ahead and put out all the utensils. If you have them, why not use them? Your table will look spectacular. The utensil to be used first goes on the outside, continuing in toward the plate in order of intended use. Line up utensils evenly at the bottom.

Check out the following list of utensils and where they should be placed as you set your table.

Side of the plate	Utensil
Left	Outside in — fish fork, salad fork, dinner fork. If you are serving European style (serving salad last), reverse the dinner and salad forks.
Right	Outside in — soup spoon, fish knife, dinner knife.

(continued)

Side of the plate	Utensil
Top	Dessert spoon and fork (with the fork closest to the plate and the handle pointing to the left, and the spoon beyond the fork with the handle pointing to the right). If you prefer, you can bring the dessert utensils in with the dessert instead of putting them on the table at the beginning of the meal.

Unless you don't mind people smoking during the meal, don't put ashtrays on the tables. Smokers, unite — outside.

Coming Up with a Seating Arrangement

Don't let slapdash seating sink your soirée. When the responses are in and you know who's coming, take time to think about guests' individual interests, and who may enjoy the company of whom.

When you decide how and where to seat your guests, consider these tips:

✔ **Seat guests at round tables, if possible.** A circle is more conducive to conversation than square or rectangular shapes. A round table also eliminates the need to choose who to seat at the head of the table.

✔ **Seat male and female guests alternately, if possible.** But don't worry if you have an uneven number of men and women.

✔ **Seat people together who have a common interest (hometown, job, hobby, or grandchildren, for example).**

✔ No matter how many tables you have, seat a male guest of honor to the right of the hostess and a female guest of honor to the right of the host.

✔ **Seat only one dominant, energetic person per table.** One table cannot handle two Dennis Rodmans. They'll clash, and your party atmosphere will collapse, fizzle, or erupt. Stars like to be stars.

✔ **Seat a very large person or any person who may have special needs (wheelchair, crutches, and so on) at the corner or end of the table.** This arrangement is more comfortable for that person and avoids possibly dividing the conversation because other guests can't see each other.

✔ **Spread shy people and good listeners among tables.**

✔ **Seat a guest who has never been to your house before in a place of honor — to the right of the host or hostess — as a thoughtful gesture.**

✔ **Don't seat husbands and wives together unless they are newlyweds.** They have plenty of opportunities to talk to each other at home. By separating them, each is free to share stories the other has heard a thousand times. You end up with two individuals contributing to conversations instead of a couple collaborating on the same topics.

✔ **Seat a handsome bachelor next to a woman who has been married 40 years.** It will be fun for both of them.

Being a Good Host

Good manners are never fussy or pretentious. Good manners put people at ease. If you are the host, manners begin with making your guests comfortable. But that won't happen if you're a bundle of nerves. So start with yourself. Forget about impressing people. Forget about what others may think. When you stop worrying about other people's opinions and judgments, you are suddenly free — free to serve the kind of food you enjoy, play the music you like, and invite the people who make you comfortable. When you clear out the worries, good manners come naturally.

Greeting guests

If you want to bring out the best in your guests, start with a warm welcome. Greet guests as you would want to be greeted, with a firm handshake or a warm hug. However you choose to greet guests, tell each person how happy you are that he or she could come. When guests feel that you are thrilled to see them, you will get the most out of their personalities.

During the first ten minutes of your party, make each guest feel like a VIP:

- ✔ Greet each person enthusiastically.

- ✔ Put guests at ease by offering drinks.

- ✔ Introduce guests to each other.

- ✔ Initiate conversations and find common ground so that guests can continue talking without you.

At the beginning of the party, unless guests are good friends or you invite them to watch or help, beware of abandoning them and disappearing into the kitchen. If guests don't know each other well, they need you to keep conversations started and flowing.

When all the guests have been greeted and are engaged in conversations, refill drinks and pass hors d'oeuvres. Even if you have hired help, passing something yourself is a good way to ensure that you get around to talking with all the guests and a way for you to gauge how conversations are faring. By passing food, you also give guests who are involved in conversations a polite way of indulging their appetites without having to interrupt the conversation and move to a food table.

Making guests comfortable with food

A common saying is "The fastest way to the heart is through the stomach." For a completely different approach to your menu, try planning it to make a particular someone happy. You can please yourself, your guests, or one special guest.

The easiest choice and one of the most common ways to make a menu is from your own viewpoint. What foods make _you_ happy? What do you like to cook? What do you want to experiment with?

Choosing foods that you love to cook and eat is a practical and delightful solution to making a menu. This approach makes perfect sense because you know what you like and you know what you are comfortable cooking. If you enjoy eating the food you serve, most likely, the guests will, too. A menu that pleases you will always be successful.

Do you have a secret recipe for lasagna? Is your cheese soufflé the envy of the neighborhood? Are you the best barbecue chef in town? There is nothing wrong with serving your specialty every time you have guests. Actually, it's a brilliant idea because it simplifies your life. People will adore eating your famous dish and will look forward to having it again.

If repeatedly using the same recipes bores you, and if you are a confident cook, take the plunge and experiment. Trying new foods on your guests is exciting — it's a challenge for you, and it's fun for the guests. When you enjoy cooking, your guests can be happy guinea pigs.

Although pleasing yourself is certainly gratifying, you may find it even more rewarding when you plan a menu with your guests' pleasure in mind. Think about whom you are serving. Suppose that you are entertaining very sophisticated world travelers who are accustomed to eating exotic foods. Consider serving them "comfort food" — plain, ordinary home cooking, such as chicken soup, beef brisket, meatloaf, apple pie, and chocolate chip cookies. Your cosmopolitan guests will be surprised and grateful for the familiar tastes of home.

On the contrary, if you are serving someone known to be the meat and potatoes type, serve what he likes, but give him a little jolt by offering one course that is unusual, such as cold kiwi soup, edible flowers, sea urchins, or cardamom ice cream.

If the thought of trying to please all your guests seems overwhelming, you may want to concentrate on pleasing one particular guest — a special guest, someone you adore, or someone you really want to impress. A unique way to make a menu and one of the best ways to honor a guest is to offer to serve his or her favorite foods. Call the guest and tell her you want to cook her favorite meal. Ask her to provide the menu.

The fact that you are willing to take the time and trouble to create someone else's favorite meal is a gesture that person will never forget.

Most people are very surprised when asked for their favorite menu and may not answer right away. However, don't take their reticence for displeasure. Instead, they are taking your question seriously and are already getting excited about coming to your party. Give them a little time to think about their special menu.

Some answers may relieve you. Others may intimidate or make you anxious. People are looking to recall a certain taste or feeling. The feeling may be easier to recreate than the specific taste because of a "secret ingredient" from an old family recipe that you don't know about. If the dish is so retro that you don't have the foggiest idea what it is and cannot even find a recipe for it, you may have to adapt something you are familiar with and know how to cook. The key is to listen to what the person wants and to match the meal as closely as possible to the guest's specific requests.

Moving your guests to the table

Getting people to the table can be one of the most frustrating parts of entertaining. You've made all this great food, it's hot, and no one is budging. Instead of getting flustered, try one of these people-moving strategies:

 ✔ At a small dinner party, ask a friend or two to take another guest and lead him or her to the table. Give the slowpokes a job. Ask them to pour wine or light the candles.

✔ At buffets or cocktail buffets, ask a female guest (the guest of honor, the oldest woman, or a close friend) to start serving herself. Then gather up some more guests. After a few people start moving in the food direction, others will follow.

✔ At large parties, moving 50 to 75 people to their tables can take 30 to 45 minutes. You and your help can tell guests, "Bring your drinks; it's time to go in; dinner's ready." Be prepared to repeat frequently.

The way you serve the food also plays a role in making your guests comfortable. Unless the party is casual, think twice before serving something messy or difficult to eat. At a cocktail or stand-up party, keep the hors d'oeuvres bite-sized so that guests can eat without making a mess of themselves. Serve drippy, greasy, sticky, or fishy foods on skewers or picks. If you do that, make sure that guests have a place to deposit the picks. You can provide a receptacle on the tray or have someone circulating through the crowd to collect them.

Following are a few tips on serving etiquette for sit-down meals. These guidelines represent traditional ways of serving. Most of these "rules" have a reason and are based on logic, common sense, and a desire for everyone to be comfortable. For example, because most people are right-handed, food is served from the left to avoid awkward body movements from the server to the guest and lessen the possibility of a plate of food landing in the guest's lap.

✔ Serving drinks from the right makes sense because the glasses are on the right side of each place setting. (If you slip up and serve a plate or pour a drink from the wrong side, or if you just like being a rebel, guests probably won't care.)

✔ Serve platters of food from the guest's left side.

✔ If you are plating food in the kitchen, you can have it on the table before guests sit down, serve it while they are sitting down, or wait until they are seated and serve it from the left.

✔ Pour drinks from the right.

✔ Don't begin clearing until everyone is finished.

✔ Clear the plates from the guest's right.

When the meal is over, whether you want guests to leave the table is strictly a judgment call. There is no right or wrong way. When guests are relaxed, content, and engaged in conversations, there is no reason why you can't continue sitting around the table.

On other occasions, moving people away from the table can be desirable:

✔ If conversation is fading and you want to inject new energy into your party

✔ If you want to create a transition between the dinner and time to leave (Some guests may be uncomfortable leaving the party directly from the table.)

✔ If you have hired help and want them to begin cleaning up

The most effective and polite way to get guests moving is to say, "Dessert and coffee will be served in the living room." If the dessert and coffee have already been served, say, "Let's move into the living room to talk."

Vamoose!: Getting your guests to go home

After dessert and coffee, guests usually linger a while longer and start their good-byes. If you are tired and ready for guests to leave, make a big deal of the first guest leaving. Stay on your feet so others get the idea that it's time to go home. (If you plop right down and get another drink, the remaining guests may follow your lead.) If you want people to leave, you must send the right signals:

✔ Stop serving drinks.

✔ Turn the music off.

✔ Let the conversation gradually subside. (Stop initiating new topics.)

✔ If you are sitting down, stand up.

✔ Tell guests how much you enjoyed having them.

✔ Don't say "no." If someone suggests that it's late and they really must go, agree with them and usher them to the door.

If guests don't pick up on these signals, you may want to try something a little less subtle. You can look at your watch and say, "Oh my gosh. Look at the time! Let's do this again soon." Or say to your spouse, "Let's go to bed and let all these nice people go home."

Many times, all the guests will leave except one or two who settle in for the long haul. For some reason, they don't get the hint. If you are a night owl, perhaps you won't mind. But if you can barely keep your eyes open, you have every right to say that you're tired. You don't need to apologize.

Don't start cleaning up until the guests have left. If it's late and you are too tired to do it all, put away the food. You can do the rest in the morning. Cleaning up makes the guests feel uncomfortable and ruins the atmosphere of the party.

Even if they offer or insist, don't let your guests wash dishes or clean up. You have made them comfortable from your invitation right up to the end of the party. Allowing them to participate in the dirty work can spoil the whole thing.

The exception is when you have cooked a holiday meal for family and close friends. You'd be crazy not to accept offers to help clear the dishes and clean up afterward.

Coping with relatives

Holiday alert: Your relatives know where you live. If you can't run away, you may as well be prepared. Some people welcome visits with relatives as a chance to strengthen family ties. Others dread them because of the stress they feel after a few days of forced togetherness. If you find family visits just slightly more agreeable than a rush-hour traffic jam, you can do more than just grin and bear it.

One solution is to keep everyone busy and productive so that there's less time to get on each other's nerves. Take advantage of their presence by letting them do some of your work. Think of different jobs for different personalities. Ask a quiet or shy person to shell peas, polish silver, or iron linens. Solicit energetic or hyperactive guests to play with the children outside. Send the most obnoxious person to the grocery store and to do the daily errands.

Cooking for a house full of relatives can be difficult if too many well-meaning helpers overrun your kitchen. For best results, do the thinking part ahead of time. Make lists, measure out ingredients, and set timers so that you don't wind up ruining the food and your mood.

If you have a visiting relative who is difficult to be around, find a polite way to keep that person out of the kitchen when you are cooking. Build a fire in the fireplace or suggest an activity that creates a focal point other than under your feet.

Planning Activities to Keep Your Guests Busy

Holiday parties are a good time to plan a special activity, use entertainment, or ask something of your guests. Your objective is to grab guests' attention and get them into the spirit of the holiday.

The following are a few examples of activities to heighten your guests' joy:

- ✔ **Thanksgiving:** If the weather permits, do something outdoors. Instead of having half the people slaving in the kitchen and the other half sitting in front of the TV, organize walks, touch football, or feeding of the local ducks.

- ✔ **Christmas:** Hire singers with beautiful voices to dress up in costume and become Dickens-era carolers. Have them sing as guests are arriving. Or ask someone to lead guests in carols around the piano. You can also invite Santa Claus to make an appearance and pass out small gifts.

- ✔ **Hanukkah:** Bring families together to celebrate. Children can play dreidel games and exchange Hanukkah *gelt* (chocolate "coins" wrapped in gold foil) or make menorahs out of nuts and bolts. (Use nuts for candleholders.)

✔ **Kwanzaa:** Ask guests to dress in traditional African attire. Arrange Kwanzaa symbols and decorations, conduct a candle-lighting ceremony, sing the Kwanzaa song, and provide children with materials for making homemade gifts to exchange.

✔ **New Year's Eve:** Ask guests to wear hats for a Mad Hatter's party. Besides the fun of looking outrageous, guests can win prizes for their efforts and steal kisses under their hat brims. Or engage guests' imaginations. Give a New Year's Eve century party. Ask each person to dress in the fashion of one of the decades in the past century.

Part II
Cooking Up a Storm

The 5th Wave   By Rich Tennant

"We're currently in a state of weightlessness. Amazingly, everything has begun floating *except* Doug's fruitcake."

In this part...

*I*n this part, we tackle a major part of holiday entertaining: food. Whether you're hosting a cocktail party or a family dinner, we have the recipes in this part that will do the trick, including a great dish for your favorite vegetarian. And if you're not sure what kind of drinks to serve, we provide some great recipes here as well.

Drinks, appetizers, main courses, side dishes, and desserts — everything you need to make a great meal is in this part.

Chapter 4

The Dinner — From Salad to Main Course

In This Chapter

▶ Serving up a mean salad

▶ Choosing and preparing a main course

▶ Remembering the side dishes

*F*ood is a huge part of the holidays. And if you're throwing a holiday party and you're not quite sure where to start, look no farther. In this chapter, we give you some fantastic recipes for traditional holiday meals as well as some alternatives for excitement. If you can't figure out what to feed your favorite vegetarian, we include several great recipes for you. And we even give you a recipe for one dish that can serve as an entire meal (it can't get much easier than that!). Salads, main courses, side dishes — they're all here in this chapter. So pick and choose what you and your guests will enjoy, and have fun cooking!

Starting with Salads

Salads are often overlooked in the meal-planning process, but they set the tone for the entire meal, so don't forget to think about what kind of salad you want to serve. In this section, we give you a recipe for a basic salad that goes well with any dish. We also give you three quick recipes for throwing together a salad that's sure to please your guests.

Making a basic salad

If you're looking for a basic, well-balanced salad recipe, read on.

Mixed Green Salad with Red Onion

Tools: *Large pot, salad spinner or paper towels, chef's knife, small mixing bowl*

Preparation time: *About 20 minutes*

Yield: *4 servings*

4 cups Boston or red-leaf lettuce leaves	*1½ tablespoons red or white vinegar*
3 cups arugula	*Salt and freshly ground pepper to taste*
⅓ cup peeled and coarsely chopped red onion	*¼ cup olive oil*
2 tablespoons finely chopped fresh parsley	

1 Rinse the greens in a large pot of cold water. (Change the water several times, rinsing until no sand remains and the greens are thoroughly cleaned.) Pick over the leaves, removing tough stems. Spin the greens in a salad spinner or lay them flat on paper towels and pat dry. (Greens may be washed and dried ahead of serving time and stored in plastic bags in the refrigerator.)

2 Tear the washed and dried greens into bite-sized pieces and put them in a salad bowl; then add the onion and parsley.

3 Put the vinegar in a small mixing bowl and add salt and pepper. Start beating while gradually adding the oil. Pour the dressing over the salad and toss to blend well.

Whipping up three quick salads

If you're in the mood to be creative but you don't have much time, create one of your own salads from these simple combinations:

- ✔ **Tomato, red onion, and basil salad:** Slice ripe, red tomatoes ¼ inch thick and layer on a platter with diced red onion and 4 or 5 large chopped fresh basil leaves. Drizzle with oil and vinegar and season with salt and pepper.

- ✔ **Red and green pepper rice salad:** Combine about 3 cups cooked white rice with 1 cup cooked green peas and 2 cups seeded, cored, and chopped red, green, or yellow peppers (or any combination of colors). Toss with enough herb-vinaigrette dressing to moisten the ingredients sufficiently, add salt and pepper to taste, and chill before serving.

- ✔ **Cherry tomato and feta cheese salad:** Toss 1 pint cherry tomatoes, rinsed and sliced in half, with 4 ounces crumbled feta cheese and ½ cup sliced, pitted black olives. Season with vinaigrette dressing to taste.

Making the Main Course

Deciding what to make for the main course of your holiday meal can be overwhelming. So in this section we give you recipes for a traditional turkey dinner, a meal you can make in one pot, and one that works well for vegetarians.

Roasting a turkey

The strict definition of *roasting* is cooking in an oven in which heat emanates from the walls and air circulates slowly around.

The art of roasting is 90 percent timing and 10 percent patience. And if you use a meat thermometer when roasting meats, fouling up is almost impossible.

Check the label on your turkey for approximate cooking times and temperatures. Remove the turkey from the oven when its internal temperature is 5 to 10 degrees *less* than the final internal temperature, and then let it rest for 15 to 20 minutes. During the resting time, the turkey cooks 5 to 10 degrees more. None of this is exact science, though; you have to use a meat thermometer to get the results you like. See Figure 4-1 for illustrated instructions for using a meat thermometer.

Where to Put a Dial (or Oven-proof) Meat Thermometer

Turkey

*For an accurate reading, do NOT touch the bone, fat, or bottom of the pan with the thermometer

Insert inside of the thigh.

Figure 4-1: How to insert a meat thermometer in a turkey.

When inserting a meat thermometer in a roast, do not let the metal touch the bone — the bone is hotter than the meat and registers a falsely higher temperature.

If you want your turkey to hold its shape perfectly while roasting, you can truss it. You can do without this step, if you're in a hurry, but we explain the technique anyway. Refer to Figures 4-2 and 4-3 for illustrated instructions.

Trussing a Turkey

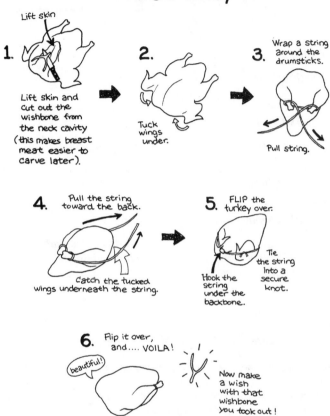

1. Lift skin

Lift skin and cut out the wishbone from the neck cavity (this makes breast meat easier to carve later).

2. Tuck wings under.

3. Wrap a string around the drumsticks.

Pull string.

4. Pull the string toward the back.

Catch the tucked wings underneath the string.

5. FLIP the turkey over.

Hook the string under the backbone.

Tie the string into a secure knot.

6. Flip it over, and.... VOILA!

beautiful!

Now make a wish with that wishbone you took out!

Figure 4-2: Trussing helps a turkey keep its shape.

Even Quicker... Truss Me!

1. Tuck wings under as in step 2, "Trussing a Turkey."

2. Cross drumsticks, and tie together.

3. Tie another string around the bird at its wings.

Figure 4-3: How to truss a turkey the fast way.

Thanksgiving
Roasted Turkey

Tools: *Chef's knife, large roasting pan*

Preparation time: *20 minutes*

Cooking time: *3 hours and 15 minutes*

Yield: *12 to 16 servings*

12- to 13-pound turkey with neck

1 onion, about ½ pound, peeled and cut into eighths

1 tablespoon peeled and finely minced garlic, about 3 large cloves

¼ pound carrots, coarsely chopped, about 4 to 5 medium carrots

Salt and pepper to taste

3 tablespoons corn, peanut, or vegetable oil

3 cups rich turkey or chicken broth

¼ cup peeled and finely chopped onion

1 Preheat the oven to 450° F.

2 Cut off and discard the wing tips of the turkey.

3 Rinse the turkey cavity well and pat dry. Stuff the cavity of the turkey with the onion pieces, garlic, carrot, and salt and pepper to taste. Sprinkle the outside of the turkey with salt and pepper and rub the turkey all over with 2 tablespoons of the oil.

4 Rub the bottom of a large roasting pan with the remaining 1 tablespoon of oil.

5 Truss the turkey with string, if desired. (See Figures 4-2 and 4-3 for instructions.)

6 Place the turkey on one side in the roasting pan. Place in the oven and roast for about 40 minutes. Turn the turkey onto its opposite side. Return it to the oven and roast for another 45 minutes, basting often.

7 When a meat thermometer registers 180° F in the thigh, remove the turkey and set it aside briefly. Pour off and discard the fat from the pan.

(continued)

8 Return the turkey to the pan, breast-side up, and return to the oven. Pour 2 cups of the broth around the turkey. Bake for about 30 minutes, turning the pan laterally so that the turkey cooks evenly. Continue baking, basting occasionally, for about 1 hour and 15 minutes. Remove the turkey from the pan and cover it loosely with aluminum foil.

9 Untruss the turkey (if necessary), cutting the string with a sharp knife or kitchen shears.

10 Scoop out the vegetables from the cavity of the turkey and add them to the liquid in the roasting pan. Add the remaining 1 cup of broth and the chopped onions, bring to a boil, and then remove from the heat. Strain the sauce and season well.

11 Carve the turkey into serving pieces, as shown in Figure 4-4, and serve with the hot pan juices.

Carving a Turkey

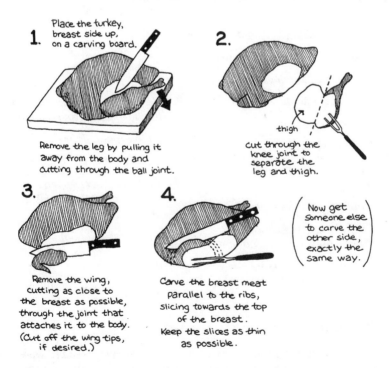

1. Place the turkey, breast side up, on a carving board. Remove the leg by pulling it away from the body and cutting through the ball joint.

2. Cut through the knee joint to separate the leg and thigh. thigh

3. Remove the wing, cutting as close to the breast as possible, through the joint that attaches it to the body. (Cut off the wing tips, if desired.)

4. Carve the breast meat parallel to the ribs, slicing towards the top of the breast. Keep the slices as thin as possible.

Now get someone else to carve the other side, exactly the same way.

Figure 4-4: How to carve a turkey.

A one-pot meal: Making a Shepherd's Pie

In Ireland, the classic Shepherd's Pie is made with beef, not lamb. We prefer the more distinctive flavor of lamb, so we're giving the following lamb recipe. If you want to try it with beef, simply substitute the same amount of meat.

This dish is so good that you may want to have leg of lamb every week just to generate enough leftovers for a pie. Some people like to add sliced carrots, leeks, or other vegetables. Try this version first and see what you think.

Shepherd's Pie

Tools: Chef's knife, large pot, potato masher or ricer, large skillet, ovenproof dish

Preparation time: About 45 minutes

Baking time: About 35 minutes

Yield: 4 to 6 servings

2½ pounds baking potatoes

4 tablespoons butter

About 1 cup milk

Salt and freshly ground pepper to taste

1 tablespoon vegetable oil

½ cup peeled and chopped onion, about 1 medium onion

2 teaspoons peeled and chopped garlic, about 2 large cloves

1½ pounds cooked, chopped lamb (or raw, ground lamb)

1 tablespoon flour

½ cup beef or chicken stock

1 tablespoon chopped fresh thyme or sage, or 1 teaspoon dried

1 tablespoon chopped fresh rosemary leaves, or 1 teaspoon dried

Dash of nutmeg

1 Preheat the oven to 350° F.

2 Peel and quarter potatoes. Bring a large pot of lightly salted water to a boil. Add the potatoes and cook, covered, until potatoes are tender, about 20 minutes. Drain well and return the potatoes to the pot.

(continued)

3 Mash the potatoes with a masher or ricer along with 2 tablespoons of the butter and enough milk to make them smooth and fluffy. Season with salt and pepper and set aside.

4 Heat the oil in a large skillet over medium-low heat. Add the onion and garlic and cook, stirring, until the onion is soft and wilted. (Be careful not to let the garlic brown.) Turn up the heat to medium and add the lamb. Cook about 5 minutes, stirring. (If using raw, ground lamb, cook 10 to 15 minutes or until it is rare.) Pour off and discard any fat in the pan.

5 Add the flour and cook, stirring, for about 2 to 3 minutes. Add the stock, thyme, rosemary, nutmeg, and salt and pepper. Reduce the heat to low and simmer, stirring occasionally, for about 15 minutes. Remove from the heat and let cool slightly.

6 Transfer the lamb mixture to an oval gratin dish (about 9 inches long) or a pie plate. Spread the mashed potatoes over everything. Dot with the remaining 2 tablespoons butter (which simply means to break up the butter into several small pieces and distribute it evenly) and bake for 35 minutes or until nicely browned. Let cool for 5 minutes before serving.

Including vegetarians in your holiday meal

If you're a vegetarian or you'll be entertaining one at your holiday party, be sure to prepare something special as a main course or an alternative to your meat dish. Expecting vegetarians to make do by just eating salad and side dishes doesn't do much to help them enjoy the meal. Try the following recipe, which is sure to be enjoyed by everyone at your dinner table, not just the vegetarians.

Fettuccine with Goat Cheese and Asparagus

Tools: *Large pot, large skillet, colander, grater*

Preparation time: *About 15 minutes*

Cooking time: *About 20 minutes*

Yield: *4 servings*

(continued)

Water

Salt to taste

1¼ pounds fresh asparagus

4 ripe plum tomatoes

¾ pound fettuccine

2 tablespoons olive oil

2 tablespoons butter

2 teaspoons peeled and finely chopped garlic, about 2 large cloves

¼ pound soft goat cheese

¼ cup coarsely chopped fresh basil leaves

Freshly ground pepper to taste

Freshly grated Parmesan cheese (optional)

1 Bring 4 to 5 quarts lightly salted water to a boil in a large, covered pot over high heat.

2 Meanwhile, remove the woody base of the asparagus with a knife or by snapping at the natural breaking point (about 2 inches from the thick, woody end). Slice the spears diagonally, creating ½-inch pieces. Rinse and drain well.

3 Remove the core of the tomatoes. Cut an "X" on the bottom of the tomatoes. When the water boils, carefully drop the tomatoes into the water for 10 to 20 seconds. Remove them from the water with a long-handled fork or a slotted spoon. (You are cooking them only long enough to loosen the skins.) Immerse the tomatoes in a bowl of cold water. When they are cool enough to handle, peel off the skins with a paring knife. Remove the seeds. Chop the tomatoes coarsely and set aside. (Refer to Figure 4-5 for illustrated instructions of this entire step.)

4 Bring the water to a boil again and add the fettuccine. Stir thoroughly to separate the strands and cook, uncovered, for about 8 minutes or just until *al dente* (the tender but still firm texture of perfectly cooked pasta).

5 As the pasta cooks, heat the oil and butter in a large skillet and add the asparagus, tomatoes, and garlic. Cook over medium heat for 4 to 5 minutes, stirring, until the asparagus is crisp-tender. Reduce heat to very low to keep warm.

6 Before draining the pasta, use a measuring cup to carefully scoop out and reserve ¼ cup of the cooking liquid. When it's ready, drain the pasta and return it to the large pot.

7 Add the vegetable mixture, goat cheese, basil, and salt and pepper to the pasta. Toss well over medium heat just until warmed through. If the sauce needs extra liquid, pour in some of the reserved cooking water. Serve immediately with Parmesan cheese on the side, if desired.

How to Peel, Seed, and Chop Tomatoes

Figure 4-5: How to peel, seed, and chop tomatoes.

Serving Up Side Dishes

Side dishes add a lot to any meal, and in this section we give you some traditional side dish recipes as well as one you can try if you want something new and different.

Honoring tradition: Mashed potatoes

When it comes to mashing potatoes, the slow way is the best. Mashed potatoes are much better when mashed by hand with a potato masher or fork or when pressed through a *ricer* (a round, metal device with small holes through which foods are pressed). Blenders and food processors whiz too fast and can leave you with excellent wallboard paste. Even when mashing by hand, don't overdo it. Mash just enough to get rid of the lumps.

Keep in mind that the following recipe calls for Idaho potatoes. Though it sounds like a contradiction, Idaho potatoes (officially called "baking" potatoes) actually make fluffier, lighter mashed potatoes than "boiling" potatoes do. Boiling potatoes get dense and gluey when they are mashed but are great for recipes in which they need to hold their shape — such as in potato salad.

Mashed Potatoes

Tools: *Chef's knife, medium saucepan fitted with a lid, potato masher or ricer, colander*

Preparation time: *About 15 minutes*

Cooking time: *About 20 minutes*

Yield: *4 servings*

4 large Idaho potatoes, about 2 pounds

½ teaspoon salt, or to taste

3 tablespoons butter

½ cup milk

Freshly ground pepper to taste

1 Peel the potatoes and cut them into quarters.

2 Place them in a medium saucepan with cold water to barely cover and add ½ teaspoon salt, or to taste.

3 Cover and bring to a boil over high heat. Reduce heat to medium and cook, covered, for about 15 minutes or until you can easily pierce the potatoes with a fork.

4 Drain the potatoes in a colander and then return them to the saucepan. Shake the potatoes in the pan over low heat for 10 to 15 seconds to evaporate excess moisture, if necessary.

5 Remove the pan from the heat. Mash the potatoes a few times with a potato masher, ricer, or fork. (You can use a hand-held mixer to mash them on low speed if you don't have a potato masher, but be careful not to overdo it!) Add the butter, milk, and salt and pepper to taste and mash again until smooth and creamy.

For garlic mashed potatoes, wrap a whole, medium head of garlic in aluminum foil and roast it in a 350° F oven for 1 hour. Remove the foil, allow the cloves to cool slightly, and then press the soft cloves free of their crispy skins. Mash them into the potatoes with the butter and milk; then season with salt and pepper to taste. You can mash other cooked vegetables, such as broccoli, carrots, turnips, or sweet potatoes, into the potatoes to add flavor and color.

Making wild rice

Wild rice is a remote relative of white rice and is actually a long-grain, aquatic grass. The wild version (it is now cultivated) grows almost exclusively in the Great Lakes region of the United States and has become quite expensive because of its scarcity. You can reduce the expense of wild rice by cooking and combining it with brown rice.

Wild rice is especially good with robust meat dishes, game, and smoked foods.

Basic Wild Rice

Tools: *Colander, medium saucepan fitted with a lid*

Preparation time: *About 15 minutes*

Cooking time: *About 50 minutes*

Yield: *4 to 6 servings*

1 cup wild rice	2 tablespoons butter
2½ cups water	Salt and freshly ground pepper to taste

1 Wash the wild rice thoroughly before you cook it. Place the rice in a pot filled with cold water and let stand for a few minutes. Pour off the water and any debris that floats to the surface. Drain well in a colander.

2 Bring the 2½ cups water to a boil in a medium covered saucepan over high heat. Add the rinsed rice, butter, and salt and pepper to taste. Stir once. Reduce the heat to low and simmer, covered, for 45 to 55 minutes or until the rice is tender.

3 Fluff the rice and add more salt and pepper, if desired, before serving.

Getting crazy with couscous

If you've never tried couscous, this recipe will be an eye-opener. Couscous is a wonderful alternative to rice or noodles.

Couscous, which is really *semolina* (coarse durum wheat) grains, originated in North Africa and is especially popular in Morocco, Algeria, and Tunisia. Traditional couscous is steamed over simmering meats and vegetables in a two-tier utensil called a *couscoussière*.

Precooked couscous, available in supermarkets, is quite good, too, and it saves a lot of time. Couscous is a fine alternative to rice or noodles with many foods, simply seasoned with butter, salt, and pepper. It is exceptionally tasty when you cook it in a flavorful stock, stirring well to keep the grains fluffy. We add onions, garlic, yellow squash, and coriander. Zucchini and eggplant are fine substitutes for the yellow squash.

Couscous with Yellow Squash

Tools: *Chef's knife, medium saucepan or pot fitted with a lid*

Preparation time: *About 15 minutes*

Cooking time: *About 10 minutes*

Yield: *4 servings*

1 tablespoon butter	*2 cups fresh or canned chicken or vegetable broth*
1 tablespoon olive oil	
⅓ cup peeled and finely chopped onion, about 1 small onion	*1 cup precooked couscous*
	¼ cup coarsely chopped fresh coriander
1 teaspoon peeled and finely chopped garlic, about 1 large clove	*Salt and freshly ground pepper to taste*
1 cup diced yellow squash, cut into ¼-inch cubes, about 1 small squash	

1 Heat the butter and oil in a medium saucepan over medium heat. Add the onion, garlic, and squash. Cook, stirring, over medium heat until the onion wilts, about 2 to 3 minutes.

2 Add the chicken or vegetable broth and bring to a boil. Add the couscous and blend well. Cover tightly, remove from the heat, and let
stand for 5 minutes. Stir in the coriander with a fork. Season to taste
with salt and pepper, if desired.

You can substitute 1 cup fresh or frozen cooked corn kernels
or peas for the yellow squash.

If you plan to serve this dish to vegetarians, use vegetable
broth instead of chicken broth. Some strict vegetarians don't
eat any food that has come in contact with animal products.

Chapter 5

Getting It Started and Wrapping It Up: Your Guide to Appetizers, Drinks, and Desserts

In This Chapter

▶ Putting together some great appetizers

▶ Knowing which drinks to serve your guests

▶ Winning them over with a fantastic dessert

*W*hether you're having a cocktail party or a complete dinner party, appetizers and drinks can get things off on the right foot. So in this chapter we give you several great recipes for appetizers and guide you through some popular holiday drinks. Finally, what would a book on holiday entertaining be without some fantastic dessert recipes? In this chapter, you get the scoop on baking a homemade apple pie, whipping up some hot fudge sauce that's to-die-for, and baking Christmas cookies to rival your mom's. No matter what kind of holiday shindig you're having, we provide the recipes in this chapter that will get it started and finish it off in style.

Greeting Your Guests with Quick and Easy Appetizers

In France, *tartines* are open-faced sandwiches that can be topped with cheese, meats, fish, or whatever. This tasty version calls for goat cheese and olive oil and couldn't be easier. These tidbits are superb with red wine.

Garlic and Goat Cheese Tartines

Tools: *Toaster oven (optional), bread knife*

Preparation time: *About 10 minutes*

Cooking time: *Less than a minute*

Yield: *6 to 8 servings*

½ loaf French or Italian bread, sliced into ¼-inch pieces

3 cloves garlic, peeled and split

¼ cup olive oil (about)

Salt and freshly ground pepper to taste

8 ounces fresh goat cheese

3 sprigs fresh rosemary, thyme, or sage, coarsely chopped

1 In a toaster oven or preheated 400° F oven, toast the bread slices until they just begin to turn golden, no more. Let the bread cool.

2 Rub the bread on both sides with the garlic. Drizzle about ½ teaspoon olive oil over one side of each slice. Lightly salt and pepper the same side.

3 Spread goat cheese over the slices and garnish with chopped fresh herbs.

And with a little practice, you can knock off any of these appetizers in minutes:

✔ **Hummus dip:** Whirl in a blender until smooth a 16-ounce can of drained chickpeas, 1 clove garlic, ¼ cup sesame seeds, the juice and grated peel of 1 lemon, ½ cup water, and salt and freshly ground pepper to taste. Serve on triangles of toasted pita or with assorted vegetable *crudités* (a fancy way of saying "raw vegetables served as appetizers").

✔ **Sweet mustard chicken kebobs:** Thread thin strips of boneless chicken and cherry tomatoes on skewers (if skewers are wooden, soak them first for half an hour in water); grill or broil about 2 minutes a side or until done, brushing at the last minute with store-bought honey mustard. Serve hot.

✔ **Sun-dried tomato spread:** Whirl sun-dried tomatoes, garlic, and onions in a food processor or blender container with enough oil to moisten into a coarse spread. Season with white pepper. Serve on melba toast rounds.

Serving Drinks

Most holiday parties wouldn't be complete without drinks of some sort. And in this section, we give you all the information you need — everything from punches to the all-time favorites. We even throw in a couple of recipes for people steering clear of alcohol altogether.

The one-two: Making a mean punch

Punch may have come from the word *puncheon,* a cast made to hold liquids such as beer. The word may also have come from the Hindu word *pantsh,* which means five. What does five have to do with anything? British expatriates in India in the seventeenth century made a beverage consisting of five ingredients: tea, water, sugar, lemon juice, and a fermented sap called *arrack.*

Regardless of the history or origin, punches of all kinds are an expected beverage at many of today's holiday gatherings. Try these punches to add a little kick to your holiday party.

Champagne Punch Royale

Yield: 8 servings

1 bottle Chantaine Sparkling Wine, chilled

⅓ cup Royale Montaine Cognac and Orange Liqueur

1 cup sliced strawberries

1 cup orange juice

1 small bottle club soda

2 tablespoons sugar

1 Place sliced strawberries in large bowl and sprinkle with sugar.

2 Add orange juice and Royale Montaine Cognac and Orange Liqueur.

3 Let sit for 1 hour.

4 Add the chilled sparkling wine and club soda.

Open House Punch

To save time, the first four ingredients may be mixed in advance. Add 7-Up or Sprite and ice when you're ready to serve.

Yield: 32 servings (4 ounces each)

750 mL Southern Comfort

6 ounces lemon juice

6-ounce can frozen lemonade

6-ounce can frozen orange juice

3 liters 7-Up or Sprite

Red food coloring

Orange and lemon slices

1 Chill ingredients.

2 Mix Southern Comfort, lemon juice, frozen lemonade, and frozen orange juice in punch bowl.

3 Add 7-Up or Sprite.

4 Add drops of red food coloring as desired and stir.

5 Float a block of ice and garnish with orange and lemon slices.

Knowing how to make a few popular drinks

When you're throwing a party, you need to know how to mix a few drinks for your guests. So here we give you the recipes for some of the holiday favorites. If you know how to mix these, you can't go wrong.

Baileys Irish Coffee

1 part Baileys Irish Cream

½ part Irish whiskey

4 parts freshly brewed coffee

1 tablespoon whipped sweetened cream

1 After brewing coffee, combine with Irish cream and whiskey.

2 Top with whipped cream.

Egg Nog

1¼ ounces Bacardi Light or Dark Rum

1 egg

1 teaspoon sugar

Milk

Nutmeg

1 Mix rum, egg, sugar, and milk in a shaker and strain into a glass.

2 Sprinkle with nutmeg.

Martini

2 ounces gin

Dash of extra dry vermouth

2 olives

1 Shake or stir gin and vermouth over ice.

2 Strain and serve in a cocktail glass straight up or over ice.

3 Garnish with olives.

Rum & Coke

1½ ounces rum   3 ounces Coke

1 Add rum and Coke to glass.

2 Stir with ice.

Scotch 'n' Soda

1½ ounces scotch   3 ounces club soda

1 Add scotch and club soda to glass.

2 Stir with ice.

Spritzer

3 ounces dry white wine   Lemon twist

Club soda

1 Pour wine in a glass and fill with soda.

2 Garnish with a lemon twist.

Vodka & Tonic

1½ ounces vodka   Lime wheel

3 ounces tonic

1 Stir vodka and tonic with ice in a glass.

2 Garnish with a lime wheel.

Offering up a nonalcoholic beverage

When you throw your holiday party, keep in mind those guests who may not be drinking alcohol for one reason or another. In addition to offering coffee, tea, and sodas, be able to offer one of a couple of drinks from your home bar. The two we offer here are favorites.

Shirley Temple

1 ounce Rose's Lime Juice   *6 ounces Schweppes Ginger Ale*

1 ounce Rose's Grenadine   *1 cherry*

1 Pour lime juice, grenadine, and ginger ale over ice in a tall glass.

2 Garnish with a cherry.

Virgin Mary

4 ounces tomato juice   *Dash of salt and pepper*

Dash of Worcestershire sauce   *Celery stalk*

Dash of Tabasco Sauce

1 In a glass filled with ice, add tomato juice.

2 Add a dash or two of Worcestershire sauce, Tabasco Sauce, salt, and pepper.

3 Garnish with a celery stalk.

Delighting Your Guests with Desserts

Desserts are the perfect way to end a holiday meal. And in this section we give you three great recipes to use.

Baking an apple pie that would make Grandma proud

What would the holidays be without a homemade apple pie? In this section, we give you a recipe that will make you the hit of the holiday season.

The following recipe calls for pastry dough. To save time during your already hectic holiday season, we recommend using store-bought pie crusts. Look for the crusts that *don't* come pre-molded to fit a pie pan. Instead, find the kind of crust that comes two per package in flat discs of dough that you can roll out to fit your pan. Use one crust for the bottom and one for the top.

Apple Pie

Tools: *Paring knife, large bowl, 9-inch pie plate*

Preparation time: *About 30 minutes*

Cooking time: *About 1 hour*

Yield: *6 to 8 servings*

6 medium apples (tart style is best), peeled, cored, and sliced about ½- inch thick (see Figure 5-1)

¾ cup sugar

2 tablespoons flour

1 tablespoon fresh lemon juice

½ teaspoon grated lemon peel

¾ teaspoon cinnamon

⅛ teaspoon nutmeg

9-inch pie plate covered with pastry dough plus 1 uncooked sheet of pastry dough, about 11 inches in diameter

1 tablespoon butter

2 tablespoons (more or less) milk or water (optional)

1 teaspoon (more or less) sugar (optional)

(continued)

1 Preheat oven to 450° F.

2 Combine apples, sugar, flour, lemon juice, lemon peel, cinnamon, and nutmeg in a large bowl. Toss gently to coat apples with sugar and seasonings.

3 Fill the uncooked pie shell with the apple mixture. Dot the butter over the filling in small pieces. Fit the top crust over the apples, trim off excess, and crimp edges firmly with a fork. (You may want to lightly brush the bottom rim first with water, which helps to keep the edges tightly sealed as the pie bakes.)

4 Prick the top crust several times with a fork to provide a vent for steam to escape. (For a shiny crust, use a pastry brush to brush the crust lightly with milk or water and then sprinkle 1 teaspoon sugar over it.)

5 Bake for 15 minutes. Reduce heat to 350° F and bake another 45 minutes or until the pie is brown and bubbly. Cool the pie for at least 20 minutes before serving.

Peeling and Coring an Apple

Figure 5-1: You peel and core apples before slicing them into a pie.

Making your own hot fudge sauce

This recipe for hot fudge can turn an ordinary dish of ice cream into something special. Serve it over peppermint stick ice cream throughout the holiday season.

 You can prepare this sauce up to a week ahead of time and keep it covered and refrigerated. Reheat in a double boiler or in the microwave.

Cracklin' Hot Fudge Sauce

Tools: *Sifter, saucepan, chef's knife, wooden spoon*

Preparation time: *About 15 minutes*

Cooking time: *About 5 minutes*

Yield: *About 2 cups*

1 cup powdered sugar, sifted

½ cup unsalted butter (1 stick)

½ cup heavy cream

8 ounces bittersweet chocolate, chopped

2 teaspoons vanilla extract

1 In a heavy saucepan over medium-low heat, combine the powdered sugar, butter, and cream. Stir with a wooden spoon until smooth.

2 Remove the pan from the heat and add the chocolate, stirring until smooth. Then add the vanilla and stir to blend.

 If you can't find bittersweet chocolate, substitute the more common semisweet chocolate and reduce the powdered sugar by 2 tablespoons.

Christmas cookies (Sometimes nothing else will do)

This cookie recipe is quick and easy to make. Because the dough is like putty, kids can easily roll it out without tearing it. It's also easy to use with cookie cutters. And because these cookies are flat, they're well-suited for decorating.

Christmas Cookies

Tools: *Rolling pin, cutter shapes, plastic wrap, parchment paper, pastry bag*

Preparation time: *45 minutes*

Baking time: *15 minutes*

Yield: *12 to 16 cookies, depending on size of cookie cutters*

½ cup butter (1 stick), cut into tablespoons, room temperature	2 cups cake flour
2 ¾ cups confectioners' sugar	Pinch of salt
¼ cup cold water	1 egg white
1 egg	2 teaspoons lemon juice
Zest of 1 orange	Food coloring

1 Preheat the oven to 350° F.

2 Cream the butter and ¾ cup confectioners' sugar with a mixer or by hand until smooth. Add the water, egg, and orange rind. Blend well. Add the flour and salt. Blend.

3 Spread the dough over a sheet of plastic wrap. The dough should be about an inch thick all around. Cover with another sheet and place in the freezer for 15 minutes. Meanwhile, make the icing. (See instructions for icing.)

4 On a floured surface, roll out the cookie dough (¼ inch thick). Using cookie cutters or the rim of a glass, cut out cookies. If you want, use something pointy, like a chopstick or a cocktail stirrer, to make a hole near the edge of the cookie so that you can run a string or a ribbon through it and hang it on a tree. Lay parchment paper over a baking sheet. With a flat spatula, place the cookie dough on the parchment. Bake for 12 minutes.

5 Remove from the oven and allow cookies to cool on a rack or a cool sheet pan.

(continued)

Royal Icing

1 Combine the remaining 2 cups confectioners' sugar, egg white, and 2 teaspoons lemon juice in a mixing bowl. Blend for a minute, scraping the beaters and the bowl. (Whisking takes about 10 minutes.)

2 Divide the icing into 3 different bowls and add food coloring of choice to each bowl.

3 Use a pastry bag with a pencil-point tip. Fill with colored icing and draw the icing on the cookie (see Figure 5-2).

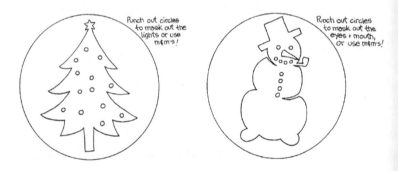

Figure 5-2: Ways to decorate your cookies.

Part III
The Part
of Tens

The 5th Wave   By Rich Tennant

"Oh, will you take that thing off before
you embarrass someone!"

In this part...

*T*his is the fun part of the book. Here we offer suggestions for cleaning up your house for spur-of-the-
moment company — tips that are always good to know.
We also provide ways to cure some common holiday
ailments and problems, including headaches, hangovers, and weight gain.

Chapter 6

Ten Ways to Clean Up Your House for Surprise Holiday Guests

In This Chapter

▶ Discovering quick and easy solutions for tidying up the kitchen and bath

▶ Finding easy ways to hide and sort clutter

▶ Freshening the air in no time

*T*he house is a mess, but who cares? You've just arrived home from a long day of battling the holiday crowds at the mall. You deserve a break. But just as you're about to settle down in your favorite chair, the phone rings. You hesitate . . . should you answer it? Will it be another annoying telemarketer, or someone offering you a million dollars? At the last possible moment, you jump up and get it. It's Aunt Bessie, your mom's sister. Her train got delayed, so she's going to drop in and isn't it great, she's only half a mile away. "Great," you mumble out loud. Inside you're cursing: "I knew I shouldn't have answered it!" Don't panic, you don't have time to clean what really needs cleaning, but you can fix up things so no one will notice the grime. If you can't get to all of these, pick and choose the ones you think are most important.

Shut the Doors

What they don't see won't hurt them, right? People don't have to see everything. Focus your cleaning on the few critical rooms your guests will go to (probably the bathroom, the living room, and the kitchen) and shut out the rest. Close the doors to anything unsightly — a messy cabinet, unmade beds, the basement, and so on. You can clean these later or just choose to leave them that way.

Get Rid of the Clutter

Grab a big basket or a shopping bag. Go around quickly and pick up everything that's on the floor or out of place and throw it in the basket. Hide the basket where no one will see it. This one move will improve things 100 percent.

Make Perfect Piles

Stack the magazines, books, and newspapers that are left over in nice, neat piles. Make sure you put your classy magazines on top of the piles. If things are orderly, people may think they're decorating accessories. After all, some photographers we know use stacked books for coffee tables.

Freshen the Bathroom

Take a damp paper towel and give the counter, the sink, and the toilet a quick swipe. Pick up any towels on the floor and fold them (if they're clean) or put them in the clutter basket (if they're dirty) to be dealt with later. Hang a couple of pretty guest towels (that you save just for unexpected guests) on the towel bar. Rinse out the soap dish and put in a fresh bar of soap.

Tidy Up the Kitchen

Remove any dirty plates, glasses, utensils, and platters from the countertops and stuff them in the dishwasher. Or pile them neatly in the sink if the dishwasher is full or if you aren't lucky enough to have one. You can also stuff everything in a cold oven — you just have to remember to remove them before turning on the oven the next time you cook! Get rid of any dirty kitchen towels or mitts and replace them with clean ones. Wipe off the countertop with a damp sponge.

Dust Off Anything Big

Dust on small things is easy to ignore. On something large, it can be a screaming indicator that dusting is not your favorite household chore. Check the piano, the large mirror in the hall, your black leather sofa, the TV screen, and if you spot those little particles of dirt, wipe them off quickly with a slightly damp cloth.

Make Something Sparkle

Most people notice shiny objects — whether it's a diamond ring, a silver candlestick, or a brass trophy. Spend a couple seconds polishing the brass frame on top of the TV, the silver bowl on the coffee table, or the chrome faucet. Some sparkle gives your guests the impression that your whole house is thoroughly clean. A quick wipe with a soft, lint-free cloth will probably do the trick.

Clean Off the Floor

Look around the floor and use your handheld vacuum to pick up any obvious clumps of dust or pieces of dirt. Double check around the legs of sofas, tables, and chairs — dust seems to accumulate there. Shake out the mat by the front door.

Polish the Telephone

The telephone? Yes, the telephone. Although it's often dirty, we tend to get used to the grime. And yet guests get a very up-close-and-personal look when they make a call (as they often do). Take a second to wipe off the receiver and buttons with a cloth slightly dampened with household cleaner.

Freshen the Air

For guests and for yourself, light a scented candle. It makes a room inviting and cozy in an instant. But even better, the aroma can also mask any offending garbage odor, cooking smells, or just stale air. The scents of evergreen, vanilla, or cinnamon are particularly well suited for the holiday season.

If lighting candles during the day is not your thing, give the rooms a last minute shot of fragrant room deodorizer. Or do something really simple: Open the window and let in some fresh air. (If you live in a colder climate, though, remember to shut them in a few minutes — unless you want your guests to leave!)

Chapter 7

Curing Ten Common Holiday Ailments with Herbal Remedies

. . . .

In This Chapter

▶ Finding natural ways to cure some common holiday ailments

▶ Figuring out how to prevent ailments from hitting you at the holidays

. . . .

*Y*ou're sick and you want to feel better. The holidays, though meant to bring peace, joy, and relaxation, can often bring on problems such as headaches, colds, indigestion, and hangovers, just to name a few. This chapter gives you a complete guide to using herbal remedies to get yourself on the path to physical health and well-being.

In each section, we suggest herbal remedies to these common holiday complaints and provide specific herbal formulas you can easily make at home or buy at drugstores and natural-food stores. Finally, we recommend specific healthy habits that can help ease symptoms and prevent disease in an enjoyable way.

We've crammed a lot of information into this little chapter. So whether you're sick already or you want to prevent yourself from getting sick throughout the holidays, read on.

Cold

When you're under stress and around many other people who are under stress, you're more susceptible to viruses like the common cold. And the holidays can be a stressful time. Check out these suggestions for feeling better soon.

Herbal remedies: Herbs are the best way to work with nature, while accelerating the healing process and easing symptoms. Use echinacea root and leaf to stimulate your immune system, eyebright herb to decongest, elder and yarrow flowers to help increase sweating and elimination, yerba santa leaf and osha root to stimulate your respiratory tract and help remove mucus, elder flowers to remove heat from your body, and lemon balm herb and wild indigo root to help manage the effects of the virus.

Herbal formulas: Combine 1 tablespoon each of echinacea leaf and/or root and ginger rhizome in 4 cups of water. Bring herbs and water to a boil, then simmer the mixture for 20 minutes. Drink 1 cup of the tea, 3 or 4 times daily. If you prefer, mix 1 teaspoon each of the individual tinctures in 1 cup of water and drink ½ cup, 3 or 4 times daily.

Healthy habits: Try to eat warming foods when you have a cold. Spice up your diet with garlic, onions, cayenne, and ginger to help rid your body of toxins by increasing sweating. Take a hot bath with ginger tea added at the onset of a cold to help reduce unpleasant symptoms. Do an essential oil steam by adding about 6 drops of eucalyptus oil to a bowl of steaming water, covering your head with a towel, and inhaling the steam.

Depression

The holidays are notorious for being a depressing time for many people. If you're one of those who get depressed around the holidays, check out some of these remedies that may help you get through it with a smile.

Herbal remedies: Take St. John's wort tincture or standardized extract, the most proven herbal antidepressant. Add ginkgo leaf extract to increase brain energy and metabolism, and/or red Korean or red Chinese ginseng root to increase vital energy, especially if you're over 45 or so. Use essential oil of lavender as an inhalant daily to lift your spirits.

Herbal formulas: Combine 1 teaspoon each of the tinctures of St. John's wort leaf and flower, ginkgo leaf, rosemary leaf, lavender flowers, and ½ teaspoon of red ginseng tincture in 1 cup of water, and drink ½ cup, morning and evening, away from mealtimes.

Healthy habits: Include more vegetables, fruits, and whole grains in your diet. Decrease fat intake. Make sure you're getting enough high-quality protein from fish, daily beans like tofu, and nutritional yeast, because your nervous system runs on the amino acids that you get from protein. Regular exercise, fresh air, and deep breathing are good depression busters.

Fatigue

What with all the running around you do during the holiday season, you're sure to feel tired occasionally, if not constantly, from Thanksgiving through the New Year. Check out these remedies to help you get up and running in no time.

Herbal remedies: Take ginger rhizome and eleuthero (Siberian ginseng) root internally to increase your energy and balance your digestive and hormonal systems. Herbs such as maté and green tea give you a temporary boost, but don't take them long-term, due to their caffeine content. Traditional medicine views fatigue as a common symptom of digestive weakness. Herbalists recommend taking digestive-strengthening herbs to increase the ability of your digestion to release energy from the food you eat. You can try the basic formulas we provide here to see if they help give you more natural deep energy. The first formula includes astragalus root, ginger rhizome, and red ginseng root. Take them as a tea, tincture, or extract in capsule or tablet form. The second formula is a bitters formula with one part each of ginger rhizome, cardamom seed, and artichoke leaf, and ½ part of gentian root. These single herbs and formulas that contain them are widely available in liquid tincture form. Capsules and tablets don't work as well.

Herbal formulas: Combine 1 teaspoon each of wild oats spikelets, damiana herb, ginseng root, and ginger rhizome in 3 cups of water. Bring herbs and water to a boil, then simmer the mixture for 20 minutes. Drink 1 cup of the tea, 2 or 3 times daily before meals. If you prefer, mix 1 teaspoon each of the individual tinctures in 1 cup of water and drink ½ cup, 2 times daily.

Healthy habits: Even if you feel tired, try to at least take short walks in the fresh air, and practice deep breathing down in your belly as you walk. Walk at least 20 to 30 minutes daily if you can. Gradually work up to longer, more frequent exercise, including 20 minutes of aerobic activity every other day. Avoid processed foods and don't overeat. Eat plenty of greens, grains, legumes, and lightly-steamed vegetables. Eat organic food that has lots of natural vitality and nutrients. Taking a bath with 3 or 4 drops of rosemary added is a good pick-me-up.

Hangover

You probably drink more alcohol during the holiday season than you do throughout the rest of the year. So if you experience a hangover the day after a great party, try one of these remedies to get back on track.

Herbal remedies: Take ginseng root in tincture, tea, or capsule form to regulate your digestion and balance your energy. Always take 2 tablets or capsules of milk thistle extract twice daily when you're drinking. Liver cooling and detoxifying herbs can assist your body in getting rid of toxins. We recommend dandelion leaf and root, yellow dock root, and chicory root and about half the amount of gentian root.

Herbal formulas: Simmer 1 tablespoon each of dandelion root, dandelion leaf, and a teaspoon of ginger rhizome per 3 cups of water for 20 minutes. Drink 1 cup of the cool tea, several times a day. Add 1 tablespoon of the Chinese herb kudzu when it's available.

Healthy habits: After drinking alcohol, drink as much pure water as possible to help clear the bloodstream. We recommend two 8-ounce glasses of pure water, with a little lemon added, for each drink that you've had.

Headache

Commonly caused by stress — and we all feel a little bit of that throughout the holiday season — headaches can sideline you when you don't have time to sit the bench. Check out these remedies to relieve your pain.

Herbal remedies: Take pain-relieving herbs like valerian root, Roman chamomile flowers, Jamaican dogwood, or meadowsweet herb, and/or beneficial circulatory herbs like ginger root and ginkgo leaf. You can apply peppermint or lavender oil compresses to the forehead, using 2 drops essential oil in 1 cup of water.

Herbal formulas: Mix 1 teaspoon each of wood betony leaves and flowers, ginger root, feverfew herb, passion flower herb, and periwinkle leaf (if available) for each 3 cups of water. Bring herbs and water to a boil, then steep the mixture for 20 minutes. Drink 1 cup of the tea, 2 or 3 times daily, before meals. If you prefer, mix 1 teaspoon each of the individual tinctures in 1 cup of water and drink ½ cup, 2 times daily. Feverfew is the best herb for preventing migraines. We've seen patients get results when nothing else would work, but remember to take it every day for at least four months to see whether it works for you. Take 1 capsule of the powdered herb or extract, or 1 dropperful of the liquid tincture, 2 times daily.

Use liver regulating and cooling herbs for chronic headaches or temple headaches. We get good results with the herbs boldo leaf, artichoke leaf, and dandelion root, either singly or in combination.

Healthy habits: Take hot foot baths and practice deep breathing. Exercising regularly can help prevent tension headaches. Massage of the neck, shoulders, and the area at the back of your skull often provides relief.

Heartburn

If you're like the rest of us, you probably eat too many rich foods during the holiday season. Coupled with stress, this can lead to heartburn. Take a look at the remedies we provide here to combat this common ailment.

Herbal remedies: Use soothing herbs such as marshmallow root, licorice root, ginger root, peppermint leaf, and/or chamomile flowers. Herbs to relax your intestinal tract include chamomile flowers and wild yarn root.

Herbal formulas: Simmer 1 teaspoon each of marshmallow root, licorice root, and wild yam root for every 2 cups of water. Turn off heat, add 1 teaspoon of peppermint leaf, then steep for 15 minutes. Drink 1 cup of the tea, 2 or 3 times daily, before meals. If you prefer, mix 1 teaspoon each of the individual tinctures in 1 cup of water and drink ½ cup, 2 times daily.

Healthy habits: Avoid high protein foods and overly spicy foods and emphasize grains and steamed vegetables. Try not to eat when you're emotionally upset or in a hurry. Eat slowly and chew your food well.

Indigestion

You may experience indigestion if you eat while you're stressed or in a hurry, or when you overeat. All of these are typical holiday eating situations, so you may find yourself with indigestion. Check out these remedies for indigestion, and get to feeling better soon.

Herbal remedies: Take gentian root, dandelion root, and artichoke leaf in tincture form to move the bile and increase digestion. Also use the digestion-enhancing herbs ginger rhizome, peppermint leaf, and chamomile flowers in tea form. Sprinkle cayenne powder on your food or take it in capsules.

Herbal formulas: Mix 1 teaspoon each of artichoke leaf, orange peel, hops strobiles, gentian root, and angelica root in 3 cups of water. Bring herbs and water to a boil, then simmer the mixture for 20 minutes. Drink 1 cup of the tea, 2 or 3 times daily, before meals. If you prefer, mix 1 teaspoon each of the individual tinctures in 1 cup of water and drink ½ cup, 2 times daily.

Healthy habits: Eat papaya and pineapple, which both aid digestion. Try to eat slowly, without distractions, and refrain from drinking cold beverages at mealtime. Eat small, frequent meals.

Motion Sickness

Although it may be one of the less obvious holiday ailments, if you do any traveling — whether by car, train, or plane — during the holidays, you may experience motion sickness. Take a look at these ways to combat it.

Herbal remedies: Try taking ginger capsules ½ hour before departure and then every 2 or 3 hours as needed. This herb has been shown in clinical trials to be more effective than Dramamine in reducing the tendency of nausea, vomiting, and dizziness. You can also try eating crystalized ginger or drinking ginger ale — not the kind with ginger flavoring and sugar — but the high-quality kind with real ginger available in natural-food stores.

Herbal formulas: Simmer 1 tablespoon of dried ginger rhizome for every cup of water for 10 minutes. Add 1 teaspoon of lavender flowers, and let the mixture steep for 10 minutes. Drink ½ cup to 1 cup, several times daily.

Healthy habits: Try to slow your breathing. You may also apply cool compresses to your forehead. The best pressure point for preventing and reducing nausea from motion sickness is called P6 in Chinese medicine. The point is located two finger-widths above the wrist (toward your elbow) on the inside of your wrist between the two tendons. Press hard for a minute or two as needed.

Stress

In case you haven't figured it out by now, the holidays are often a time of stress. If you find yourself stressing out sometime between the end of November and the beginning of January, check out these methods of controlling the madness.

Herbal remedies: Popular antistress herbs include eleuthero (Siberian ginseng) root and licorice root. Use calmative herbs such as California poppy flowering plant, valerian root, hops strobiles, kava root, and passion flower herb on a regular basis.

Herbal formulas: Mix 1 teaspoon each of valerian root, California poppy flowering plant, hawthorn flowers and leaves, and kava root in 4 cups of water. Bring herbs and water to a boil, then steep the mixture for 20 minutes. Drink 1 cup of the tea, 2 or 3 times daily, before meals. If you prefer, mix 1 teaspoon each of the individual tinctures in 1 cup of water and drink ½ cup, 2 times daily.

Healthy habits: Detaching from the daily pressure of life is the most important factor in stress reduction. You can do this with meditation, deep breathing, visualization, stretching, and spiritual practices. Follow a natural-foods diet with lightly steamed vegetables, grains, and legumes and a little meat if you desire. Increase your intake of raw vegetables and fruits in warmer months. Emphasize foods that nourish the adrenals such as aduki beans and yams.

Weight Gain

Most people gain at least a little weight during the holiday season. And if you have — or if you want to prevent yourself from doing so — check out these herbal remedies.

Herbal remedies: Digestive strengthening herbs are essential for successful weight management. Take bitter herbs like gentian root, centaury herb, angelica root, artichoke leaf, and wormwood leaf tea, and digestive-warming herbs like ginger rhizome and red ginseng root daily before meals. Long-term use, up to six months or more, brings the best results. Many commercial formulas with various combinations of these herbs are widely available. Take 2 capsules of cayenne fruit powder, 2 times daily, to stimulate your metabolism. You may also want to take capsules of bladderwrack thallus and guggul oleoresin to regulate metabolism and support proper thyroid activity.

Herbal formulas: Simmer 1 teaspoon each of ginger rhizome, cardamom pods, orange peel, cinnamon bark, and gentian root in 4 cups of water for 15 minutes, and let the brew steep for 15 more minutes. Drink 1 cup of the tea, 2 or 3 times daily, before meals. If you prefer, mix 1 teaspoon each of the individual tinctures in 1 cup of water and drink ½ cup, 2 times daily, before meals.

Healthy habits: Engage in regular aerobic activity, including walking, running, swimming, or biking. Do gentle stretching exercises before and after to increase your flexibility. Don't eat too late at night, and, even better, have your big meal at noon, and eat lightly in the evening. Keep starches and sugar to a minimum. Lightly increase your intake of high quality protein, and focus on all kinds of fresh raw and steamed vegetables and beans. Also keep dairy, meat, oil, nuts, and eggs to a minimum.

Index

Notes

Notes

RESOLUTION SOLUTIONS

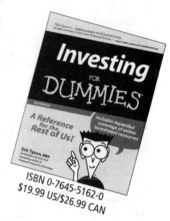

Dummies Books™
Bestsellers on Every Topic!

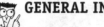 GENERAL INTEREST TITLES

BUSINESS & PERSONAL FINANCE

Accounting For Dummies®	John A. Tracy, CPA	0-7645-5014-4	$19.99 US/$27.99 CAN
Business Plans For Dummies®	Paul Tiffany, Ph.D. & Steven D. Peterson, Ph.D.	1-56884-868-4	$19.99 US/$27.99 CAN
Business Writing For Dummies®	Sheryl Lindsell-Roberts	0-7645-5134-5	$16.99 US/$27.99 CAN
Consulting For Dummies®	Bob Nelson & Peter Economy	0-7645-5034-9	$19.99 US/$27.99 CAN
Customer Service For Dummies®, 2nd Edition	Karen Leland & Keith Bailey	0-7645-5209-0	$19.99 US/$27.99 CAN
Franchising For Dummies®	Dave Thomas & Michael Seid	0-7645-5160-4	$19.99 US/$27.99 CAN
Getting Results For Dummies®	Mark H. McCormack	0-7645-5205-8	$19.99 US/$27.99 CAN
Home Buying For Dummies®	Eric Tyson, MBA & Ray Brown	1-56884-385-2	$16.99 US/$24.99 CAN
House Selling For Dummies®	Eric Tyson, MBA & Ray Brown	0-7645-5038-1	$16.99 US/$24.99 CAN
Human Resources Kit For Dummies®	Max Messmer	0-7645-5131-0	$19.99 US/$27.99 CAN
Investing For Dummies®, 2nd Edition	Eric Tyson, MBA	0-7645-5162-0	$19.99 US/$27.99 CAN
Law For Dummies®	John Ventura	1-56884-860-9	$19.99 US/$27.99 CAN
Leadership For Dummies®	Marshall Loeb & Steven Kindel	0-7645-5176-0	$19.99 US/$27.99 CAN
Managing For Dummies®	Bob Nelson & Peter Economy	1-56884-858-7	$19.99 US/$27.99 CAN
Marketing For Dummies®	Alexander Hiam	1-56884-699-1	$19.99 US/$27.99 CAN
Mutual Funds For Dummies®, 2nd Edition	Eric Tyson, MBA	0-7645-5112-4	$19.99 US/$27.99 CAN
Negotiating For Dummies®	Michael C. Donaldson & Mimi Donaldson	1-56884-867-6	$19.99 US/$27.99 CAN
Personal Finance For Dummies®, 2nd Edition	Eric Tyson, MBA	0-7645-5013-6	$19.99 US/$27.99 CAN
Personal Finance For Dummies® For Canadians	Eric Tyson, MBA & Tony Martin	1-56884-378-X	$19.99 US/$27.99 CAN
Public Speaking For Dummies®	Malcolm Kushner	0-7645-5159-0	$16.99 US/$24.99 CAN
Sales Closing For Dummies®	Tom Hopkins	0-7645-5063-2	$14.99 US/$21.99 CAN
Sales Prospecting For Dummies®	Tom Hopkins	0-7645-5066-7	$14.99 US/$21.99 CAN
Selling For Dummies®	Tom Hopkins	1-56884-389-5	$16.99 US/$24.99 CAN
Small Business For Dummies®	Eric Tyson, MBA & Jim Schell	0-7645-5094-2	$19.99 US/$27.99 CAN
Small Business Kit For Dummies®	Richard D. Harroch	0-7645-5093-4	$24.99 US/$34.99 CAN
Taxes 2000 For Dummies®	Eric Tyson & David J. Silverman	0-7645-5206-6	$14.99 US/$21.99 CAN
Time Management For Dummies®, 2nd Edition	Jeffrey J. Mayer	0-7645-5145-0	$19.99 US/$27.99 CAN
Writing Business Letters For Dummies®	Sheryl Lindsell-Roberts	0-7645-5207-4	$16.99 US/$24.99 CAN

TECHNOLOGY TITLES

WEB DESIGN & PUBLISHING

Creating Web Pages For Dummies®, 4th Edition	Bud Smith & Arthur Bebak	0-7645-0504-1	$24.99 US/$34.99 CAN
FrontPage® 2000 For Dummies®	Asha Dornfest	0-7645-0423-1	$24.99 US/$34.99 CAN
HTML 4 For Dummies®, 2nd Edition	Ed Tittel & Stephen Nelson James	0-7645-0572-6	$24.99 US/$34.99 CAN
Java™ For Dummies®, 2nd Edition	Aaron E. Walsh	0-7645-0140-2	$24.99 US/$34.99 CAN
PageMill™ 2 For Dummies®	Deke McClelland & John San Filippo	0-7645-0028-7	$24.99 US/$34.99 CAN

DESKTOP PUBLISHING GRAPHICS/MULTIMEDIA

CorelDRAW™ 9 For Dummies®	Deke McClelland	0-7645-0523-8	$19.99 US/$27.99 CAN
Desktop Publishing and Design For Dummies®	Roger C. Parker	1-56884-234-1	$19.99 US/$27.99 CAN
Digital Photography For Dummies®, 2nd Edition	Julie Adair King	0-7645-0431-2	$19.99 US/$27.99 CAN
Adobe® InDesign™ For Dummies®	Deke McClelland	0-7645-0599-8	$19.99 US/$27.99 CAN
Microsoft® Publisher 98 For Dummies®	Jim McCarter	0-7645-0395-2	$19.99 US/$27.99 CAN

Dummies Books™
Bestsellers on Every Topic!

GENERAL INTEREST TITLES

FOOD & BEVERAGE/ENTERTAINING

Title	Author	ISBN	Price
Bartending For Dummies®	Ray Foley	0-7645-5051-9	$14.99 US/$21.99 CAN
Cooking For Dummies®	Bryan Miller & Marie Rama	0-7645-5002-0	$19.99 US/$27.99 CAN
Entertaining For Dummies®	Suzanne Williamson with Linda Smith	0-7645-5027-6	$19.99 US/$27.99 CAN
Gourmet Cooking For Dummies®	Charlie Trotter	0-7645-5029-2	$19.99 US/$27.99 CAN
Grilling For Dummies®	Marie Rama & John Mariani	0-7645-5076-4	$19.99 US/$27.99 CAN
Italian Cooking For Dummies®	Cesare Casella & Jack Bishop	0-7645-5098-5	$19.99 US/$27.99 CAN
Mexican Cooking For Dummies®	Mary Sue Miliken & Susan Feniger	0-7645-5169-8	$19.99 US/$27.99 CAN
Quick & Healthy Cooking For Dummies®	Lynn Fischer	0-7645-5214-7	$19.99 US/$27.99 CAN
Wine For Dummies®, 2nd Edition	Ed McCarthy & Mary Ewing-Mulligan	0-7645-5114-0	$19.99 US/$27.99 CAN

SPORTS

Title	Author	ISBN	Price
Baseball For Dummies®	Joe Morgan with Richard Lally	0-7645-5085-3	$19.99 US/$27.99 CAN
Golf For Dummies®, 2nd Edition	Gary McCord	0-7645-5146-9	$19.99 US/$27.99 CAN
Fly Fishing For Dummies®	Peter Kaminsky	0-7645-5073-X	$19.99 US/$27.99 CAN
Football For Dummies®	Howie Long with John Czarnecki	0-7645-5054-3	$19.99 US/$27.99 CAN
Hockey For Dummies®	John Davidson with John Steinbreder	0-7645-5045-4	$19.99 US/$27.99 CAN
Tennis For Dummies®	Patrick McEnroe with Peter Bodo	0-7645-5087-X	$19.99 US/$27.99 CAN

HOME & GARDEN

Title	Author	ISBN	Price
Annuals For Dummies®	Bill Marken & NGA	0-7645-5056-X	$16.99 US/$24.99 CAN
Decks & Patios For Dummies®	Robert J. Beckstrom & NGA	0-7645-5075-6	$16.99 US/$24.99 CAN
Flowering Bulbs For Dummies®	Judy Glattstein & NGA	0-7645-5103-5	$16.99 US/$24.99 CAN
Gardening For Dummies®, 2nd Edition	Michael MacCaskey & NGA	0-7645-5130-2	$16.99 US/$24.99 CAN
Home Improvement For Dummies®	Gene & Katie Hamilton & the Editors of HouseNet, Inc.	0-7645-5005-5	$19.99 US/$26.99 CAN

TECHNOLOGY TITLES

INTERNET

Title	Author	ISBN	Price
America Online® For Dummies®, 5th Edition	John Kaufeld	0-7645-0502-5	$19.99 US/$27.99 CAN
Banking Online Dummies®	Paul Murphy	0-7645-0458-4	$24.99 US/$34.99 CAN
eBay™ For Dummies®	Roland Warner	0-7645-0582-3	$19.99 US/$27.99 CAN
E-Mail For Dummies®, 2nd Edition	John R. Levine, Carol Baroudi, & Arnold Reinhold	0-7645-0131-3	$24.99 US/$34.99 CAN
Genealogy Online For Dummies®	Matthew L. Helm & April Leah Helm	0-7645-0377-4	$24.99 US/$34.99 CAN
Internet Directory For Dummies®, 3ED Edition	Brad Hill	0-7645-0558-2	$24.99 US/$34.99 CAN
Internet Auctions For Dummies®	Greg Holden	0-7645-0578-9	$24.99 US/$34.99 CAN
The Internet For Dummies®, 6th Edition	John R. Levine, Carol Baroudi, & Margaret Levine Young	0-7645-0506-8	$19.99 US/$27.99 CAN
Investing Online For Dummies®, 2nd Edition	Kathleen Sindell, Ph.D.	0-7645-0509-2	$24.99 US/$34.99 CAN
World Wide Web Searching For Dummies®, 2nd Ed.	Brad Hill	0-7645-0264-6	$24.99 US/$34.99 CAN
Yahoo!® For Dummies®	Brad Hill	0-7645-0582-3	$19.99 US/$27.99 CAN

OPERATING SYSTEMS

Title	Author	ISBN	Price
DOS For Dummies®, 3rd Edition	Dan Gookin	0-7645-0361-8	$19.99 US/$27.99 CAN
LINUX® For Dummies®, 2nd Edition	John Hall, Craig Witherspoon, & Coletta Witherspoon	0-7645-0421-5	$24.99 US/$34.99 CAN
Mac® OS 8 For Dummies®	Bob LeVitus	0-7645-0271-9	$19.99 US/$27.99 CAN
Small Business Windows® 98 For Dummies®	Stephen Nelson	0-7645-0425-8	$24.99 US/$34.99 CAN
UNIX® For Dummies®, 4th Edition	John R. Levine & Margaret Levine Young	0-7645-0419-3	$19.99 US/$27.99 CAN
Windows® 95 For Dummies®, 2nd Edition	Andy Rathbone	0-7645-0180-1	$19.99 US/$27.99 CAN
Windows® 98 For Dummies®	Andy Rathbone	0-7645-0261-1	$19.99 US/$27.99 CAN

Dummies Books™
Bestsellers on Every Topic!

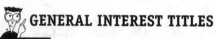

GENERAL INTEREST TITLES

EDUCATION & TEST PREPARATION

Title	Author	ISBN	Price
The ACT For Dummies®	Suzee Vlk	1-56884-387-9	$14.99 US/$21.99 CAN
College Financial Aid For Dummies®	Dr. Herm Davis & Joyce Lain Kennedy	0-7645-5049-7	$19.99 US/$27.99 CAN
College Planning For Dummies®, 2nd Edition	Pat Ordovensky	0-7645-5048-9	$19.99 US/$27.99 CAN
Everyday Math For Dummies®	Charles Seiter, Ph.D.	1-56884-248-1	$14.99 US/$21.99 CAN
The GMAT® For Dummies®, 3rd Edition	Suzee Vlk	0-7645-5082-9	$16.99 US/$24.99 CAN
The GRE® For Dummies®, 3rd Edition	Suzee Vlk	0-7645-5083-7	$16.99 US/$24.99 CAN
Politics For Dummies®	Ann DeLaney	1-56884-381-X	$19.99 US/$27.99 CAN
The SAT I For Dummies®, 3rd Edition	Suzee Vlk	0-7645-5044-6	$14.99 US/$21.99 CAN

AUTOMOTIVE

Title	Author	ISBN	Price
Auto Repair For Dummies®	Deanna Sclar	0-7645-5089-6	$19.99 US/$27.99 CAN
Buying A Car For Dummies®	Deanna Sclar	0-7645-5091-8	$16.99 US/$24.99 CAN

LIFESTYLE/SELF-HELP

Title	Author	ISBN	Price
Dating For Dummies®	Dr. Joy Browne	0-7645-5072-1	$19.99 US/$27.99 CAN
Making Marriage Work For Dummies®	Steven Simring, M.D. & Sue Klavans Simring, D.S.W	0-7645-5173-6	$19.99 US/$27.99 CAN
Parenting For Dummies®	Sandra H. Gookin	1-56884-383-6	$16.99 US/$24.99 CAN
Success For Dummies®	Zig Ziglar	0-7645-5061-6	$19.99 US/$27.99 CAN
Weddings For Dummies®	Marcy Blum & Laura Fisher Kaiser	0-7645-5055-1	$19.99 US/$27.99 CAN

TECHNOLOGY TITLES

SUITES

Title	Author	ISBN	Price
Microsoft® Office 2000 For Windows® For Dummies®	Wallace Wang & Roger C. Parker	0-7645-0452-5	$19.99 US/$27.99 CAN
Microsoft® Office 2000 For Windows®, For Dummies® Quick Reference	Doug Lowe & Bjoern Hartsfvang	0-7645-0453-3	$12.99 US/$17.99 CAN
Microsoft® Office 4 For Windows® For Dummies®	Roger C. Parker	1-56884-183-3	$19.95 US/$27.99 CAN
Microsoft® Office 97 For Windows® For Dummies®	Wallace Wang & Roger C. Parker	0-7645-0050-3	$19.99 US/$27.99 CAN
Microsoft® Office 97 For Windows® For Dummies®, Quick Reference	Doug Lowe	0-7645-0062-7	$12.99 US/$17.99 CAN
Microsoft® Office 98 For Macs® For Dummies®	Tom Negrino	0-7645-0229-8	$19.99 US/$27.99 CAN

WORD PROCESSING

Title	Author	ISBN	Price
Word 2000 For Windows® For Dummies®, Quick Reference	Peter Weverka	0-7645-0449-5	$12.99 US/$19.99 CAN
Corel® WordPerfect® 8 For Windows® For Dummies®	Margaret Levine Young, David Kay, & Jordan Young	0-7645-0186-0	$19.99 US/$27.99 CAN
Word 2000 For Windows® For Dummies®	Dan Gookin	0-7645-0448-7	$19.99 US/$27.99 CAN
Word For Windows® 95 For Dummies®	Dan Gookin	1-56884-932-X	$19.99 US/$27.99 CAN
Word 97 For Windows® For Dummies®	Dan Gookin	0-7645-0052-X	$19.99 US/$27.99 CAN
WordPerfect® 9 For Windows® For Dummies®	Margaret Levine Young	0-7645-0427-4	$19.99 US/$27.99 CAN
WordPerfect® 7 For Windows® 95 For Dummies®	Margaret Levine Young & David Kay	1-56884-949-4	$19.99 US/$27.99 CAN
Word Pro® for Windows® 95 For Dummies®	Jim Meade	1-56884-232-5	$19.99 US/$27.99 CAN

SPREADSHEET/FINANCE/PROJECT MANAGEMENT

Title	Author	ISBN	Price
Excel For Windows® 95 For Dummies®	Greg Harvey	1-56884-930-3	$19.99 US/$27.99 CAN
Excel 2000 For Windows® For Dummies®	Greg Harvey	0-7645-0446-0	$19.99 US/$27.99 CAN
Excel 2000 For Windows® For Dummies® Quick Reference	John Walkenbach	0-7645-0447-9	$12.99 US/$17.99 CAN
Microsoft® Money 98 For Dummies®	Peter Weverka	0-7645-0295-6	$24.99 US/$34.99 CAN
Microsoft® Money 99 For Dummies®	Peter Weverka	0-7645-0433-9	$19.99 US/$27.99 CAN
Microsoft® Project 98 For Dummies®	Martin Doucette	0-7645-0321-9	$24.99 US/$34.99 CAN
MORE Excel 97 For Windows® For Dummies®	Greg Harvey	0-7645-0138-0	$22.99 US/$32.99 CAN
Quicken® 98 For Windows® For Dummies®	Stephen L. Nelson	0-7645-0243-3	$19.99 US/$27.99 CAN

Dummies Books™
Bestsellers on Every Topic!

GENERAL INTEREST TITLES

HE ARTS

Art For Dummies®	Thomas Hoving	0-7645-5104-3	$24.99 US/$34.99 CAN
Blues For Dummies®	Lonnie Brooks, Cub Koda, & Wayne Baker Brooks	0-7645-5080-2	$24.99 US/$34.99 CAN
Classical Music For Dummies®	David Pogue & Scott Speck	0-7645-5009-8	$24.99 US/$34.99 CAN
Guitar For Dummies®	Mark Phillips & Jon Chappell of Cherry Lane Music	0-7645-5106-X	$24.99 US/$34.99 CAN
Jazz For Dummies®	Dirk Sutro	0-7645-5081-0	$24.99 US/$34.99 CAN
Opera For Dummies®	David Pogue & Scott Speck	0-7645-5010-1	$24.99 US/$34.99 CAN
Piano For Dummies®	Blake Neely of Cherry Lane Music	0-7645-5105-1	$24.99 US/$34.99 CAN
Shakespeare For Dummies®	John Doyle & Ray Lischner	0-7645-5135-3	$19.99 US/$27.99 CAN

HEALTH

Alternative Medicine For Dummies®	James Dillard, M.D., D.C., C.A.C., & Terra Ziporyn, Ph.D.	0-7645-5109-4	$19.99 US/$27.99 CAN
Beauty Secrets For Dummies®	Stephanie Seymour	0-7645-5078-0	$19.99 US/$27.99 CAN
Dieting For Dummies®	The American Dietetic Society with Jane Kirby, R.D.	0-7645-5126-4	$19.99 US/$27.99 CAN
First Aid For Dummies®	Charles B. Inlander & The People's Medical Society	0-7645-5213-9	$19.99 US/$27.99 CAN
Fitness For Dummies®	Suzanne Schlosberg & Liz Neporent, M.A.	1-56884-866-8	$19.99 US/$27.99 CAN
Healing Foods For Dummies®	Molly Siple, M.S. R.D.	0-7645-5198-1	$19.99 US/$27.99 CAN
Nutrition For Dummies®	Carol Ann Rinzler	0-7645-5032-2	$19.99 US/$27.99 CAN
Pregnancy For Dummies®	Joanne Stone, M.D., Keith Eddleman, M.D., & Mary Murray	0-7645-5074-8	$19.99 US/$27.99 CAN
Sex For Dummies®	Dr. Ruth K. Westheimer	1-56884-384-4	$16.99 US/$24.99 CAN
Stress Management For Dummies®	Allen Elkin, Ph.D.	0-7645-5144-2	$19.99 US/$27.99 CAN
The Healthy Heart For Dummies®	James M. Ripple, M.D.	0-7645-5166-3	$19.99 US/$27.99 CAN
Weight Training For Dummies®	Liz Neporent, M.A. & Suzanne Schlosberg	0-7645-5036-5	$19.99 US/$27.99 CAN
Women's Health For Dummies®	Pamela Maraldo, Ph.D., R.N., & The People's Medical Society	0-7645-5119-1	$19.99 US/$27.99 CAN

TECHNOLOGY TITLES

ACINTOSH

Macs® For Dummies®, 6th Edition	David Pogue	0-7645-0398-7	$19.99 US/$27.99 CAN
Macs® For Teachers™, 3rd Edition	Michelle Robinette	0-7645-0226-3	$24.99 US/$34.99 CAN
The iMac For Dummies	David Pogue	0-7645-0495-9	$19.99 US/$27.99 CAN

C/GENERAL COMPUTING

Building A PC For Dummies®, 2nd Edition	Mark Chambers	0-7645-0571-8	$24.99 US/$34.99 CAN
Buying a Computer For Dummies®	Dan Gookin	0-7645-0313-8	$19.99 US/$27.99 CAN
Illustrated Computer Dictionary For Dummies®, 3rd Edition	Dan Gookin & Sandra Hardin Gookin	0-7645-0143-7	$19.99 US/$27.99 CAN
Modems For Dummies®, 3rd Edition	Tina Rathbone	0-7645-0069-4	$19.99 US/$27.99 CAN
Palm Computing® For Dummies®	Bill Dyszel	0-7645-0581-5	$24.99 US/$34.99 CAN
PCs For Dummies®, 7th Edition	Dan Gookin	0-7645-0594-7	$19.99 US/$27.99 CAN
Small Business Computing For Dummies®	Brian Underdahl	0-7645-0287-5	$24.99 US/$34.99 CAN
Smart Homes For Dummies®	Danny Briere	0-7645-0527-0	$19.99 US/$27.99 CAN
Upgrading & Fixing PCs For Dummies®, 4th Edition	Andy Rathbone	0-7645-0418-5	$19.99 US/$27.99 CAN

Dummies Books™
Bestsellers on Every Topic!

GENERAL INTEREST TITLES

CAREERS

Cover Letters For Dummies®	Joyce Lain Kennedy	1-56884-395-X	$12.99 US/$17.99 CAN
Cool Careers For Dummies®	Marty Nemko, Paul Edwards, & Sarah Edwards	0-7645-5095-0	$16.99 US/$24.99 CAN
Job Hunting For Dummies®, 2nd Edition	Max Messmer	0-7645-5163-9	$19.99 US/$26.99 CAN
Job Interviews For Dummies®	Joyce Lain Kennedy	1-56884-859-5	$12.99 US/$17.99 CAN
Resumes For Dummies®, 2nd Edition	Joyce Lain Kennedy	0-7645-5113-2	$12.99 US/$17.99 CAN

FITNESS

Fitness Walking For Dummies®	Liz Neporent	0-7645-5192-6	$19.99 US/$27.99 CAN
Fitness For Dummies®, 2nd Edition	Suzanne Schlosberg	0-7645-5167-1	$19.99 US/$27.99 CAN
Nutrition For Dummies®, 2nd Edition	Carol Ann Rinzler	0-7645-5180-9	$19.99 US/$27.99 CAN
Running For Dummies®	Florence "Flo-Jo" Griffith Joyner & John Hanc	0-7645-5096-9	$19.99 US/$27.99 CAN

FOREIGN LANGUAGE

Spanish For Dummies®	Susana Wald	0-7645-5194-9	$24.99 US/$34.99 CAN
French For Dummies®	Dodi-Kartrin Schmidt & Michelle W. Willams	0-7645-5193-0	$24.99 US/$34.99 CAN

TECHNOLOGY TITLES

DATABASE

Access 2000 For Windows® For Dummies®	John Kaufeld	0-7645-0444-4	$19.99 US/$27.99 CAN
Access 97 For Windows® For Dummies®	John Kaufeld	0-7645-0048-1	$19.99 US/$27.99 CAN
Approach® 97 For Windows® For Dummies®	Deborah S. Ray & Eric J. Ray	0-7645-0001-5	$19.99 US/$27.99 CAN
Crystal Reports 7 For Dummies®	Douglas J. Wolf	0-7645-0548-3	$24.99 US/$34.99 CAN
Data Warehousing For Dummies®	Alan R. Simon	0-7645-0170-4	$24.99 US/$34.99 CAN
FileMaker® Pro 4 For Dummies®	Tom Maremaa	0-7645-0210-7	$19.99 US/$27.99 CAN
Intranet & Web Databases For Dummies®	Paul Litwin	0-7645-0221-2	$29.99 US/$34.99 CAN

NETWORKING

Building An Intranet For Dummies®	John Fronckowiak	0-7645-0276-X	$29.99 US/$42.99 CAN
cc: Mail™ For Dummies®	Victor R. Garza	0-7645-0055-4	$19.99 US/$27.99 CAN
Client/Server Computing For Dummies®, 2nd Edition	Doug Lowe	0-7645-0066-X	$24.99 US/$34.99 CAN
Lotus Notes® Release 4 For Dummies®	Stephen Londergan & Pat Freeland	1-56884-934-6	$19.99 US/$27.99 CAN
Networking For Dummies®, 4th Edition	Doug Lowe	0-7645-0498-3	$19.99 US/$27.99 CAN
Upgrading & Fixing Networks For Dummies®	Bill Camarda	0-7645-0347-2	$29.99 US/$42.99 CAN
Windows NT® Networking For Dummies®	Ed Tittel, Mary Madden, & Earl Follis	0-7645-0015-5	$24.99 US/$34.99 CAN